CONTEMPORARY'S

Reading

Basics

Introductory

**McGraw-Hill
Contemporary**

ISBN: 0-8092-0700-1

Published by McGraw-Hill/Contemporary,
4255 West Touhy Avenue,
Lincolnwood (Chicago), Illinois 60712-1975 U.S.A.

5 6 7 8 9 10 11 12 13 14 15 16 CUS CUS 0 9 8 7 6 5 4 3

Contents

Contents *continued*

To the Learner

If reading has never been easy for you, Contemporary's *Reading Basics* will help. The workbook will explain basic comprehension skills. The reader will let you practice those skills on a short, interesting story. *Reading Basics* will build your confidence in your ability to read.

Using Contemporary's *Reading Basics* is a good way to improve your reading comprehension skills. The workbook covers
- vocabulary words
- recalling information
- using graphic information
- constructing meaning
- extending meaning

Included in the workbook are a Pretest and a Posttest. The Pretest will help you find your reading strengths and weaknesses. Then you can use the workbook lessons to improve your skills. When you have finished the lessons and exercises, the Posttest will help you see if you have mastered those skills. Usually mastery means completing 80% of the questions correctly.

Reading Basics will help you develop specific reading skills. Each workbook is self-contained with the Answer Key at the back of the book. Clear directions will guide you through the lessons and exercises.

Each lesson in the **workbook** is divided into four parts.

A **Introduce** clearly defines, explains, and illustrates the skill. The examples prepare you for the work in the following exercises.

B **Practice** lets you work on the skill just introduced.

C **Apply** gives you a different way to practice the comprehension skill.

D **Check Up** gives a quick test on the skill covered in the lesson.

Each selection in the **reader** will let you practice reading. The article or story will grab your interest and keep you reading to the end. When you finish reading, you will
- check your understanding of the story
- apply the workbook lesson's skill to the story

How to Use This Workbook

1. Take the Pretest on pages 7–15. Check your answers with the Answer Key on page 16. Refer to the Evaluation Chart on page 16 to find which skills you need to work on.

2. Take each four-page lesson one at a time. Ask your teacher for help with any problems you have.

3. Use the Answer Key, which begins on page 217, to correct your answers after each exercise.

4. At the end of each unit, complete the Unit Review and Unit Assessment. These will check your progress. After the Unit Assessment, your teacher may want to discuss your answers with you.

5. At the end of some lessons, you will see a Read On note about a selection in the *Reading Basics* reader. Take a break from the workbook and read the story or article. Answer the comprehension questions and the skill questions at the end of the story.

6. After you have finished all five units, take the Posttest on pages 209–215. Check your answers on page 216. Then discuss your progress with your teacher.

Circle the word that is spelled correctly and best completes each sentence.

1. Two of my brothers have brown _____.

   A hare

   B hair

   C heer

   D haer

2. He sent the package to the_____ person.

   F rong

   G rwong

   H wrong

   J whong

3. The _____ train had thirty-six cars.

   A frieght

   B frate

   C frait

   D freight

4. Are you _____ the books on the shelf?

   F puting

   G putting

   H puting

   J poatting

Read the graph and circle the answer for each question.

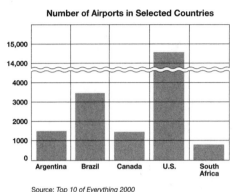

Source: *Top 10 of Everything 2000*

5. Which countries have about the same number of airports?

   A United States and Canada

   B Brazil and Argentina

   C Argentina and Canada

   D United States and Brazil

6. About how many airports does South Africa have?

   F 1770

   G 770

   H 70

   J 1400

7. Which country has about twice as many airports as Argentina?

   A Brazil

   B South Africa

   C Canada

   D United States

8. Which country has the most airports?

   F United States

   G Brazil

   H Canada

   J South Africa

Circle the answer that tells what the symbol means.

9.

A don't walk

B no left turn

C one way

D bump

10.

F pedestrian crossing

G yield

H railroad crossing

J no passing zone

11.

A hospital

B don't walk

C airport

D school

12.

F handicapped access

G no pets

H restaurant

J baggage claim

13.

A stop

B walk

C merge

D yield

14.

F bicycle route

G signal ahead

H divided highway

J no left turn

Read the map and circle the answer for each question.

SOUTH RIDGE MALL

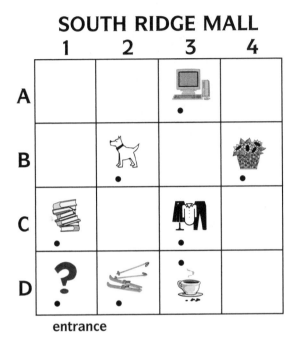

15. What does the symbol  stand for?

    A A1 Cleaners

    B Gardeners' Grove

    C The Coffee Cafe

    D Classic Books

16. What is located at coordinate D2?

    F Ski Chalet

    G Information Booth

    H Pete's Pet Shop

    J Computer Central

17. How far is it from the Coffee Cup to Computer Central?

    A 50 yards

    B 200 yards

    C 100 yards

    D 500 yards

Read each paragraph and circle the answer for each question.

Fleas are great jumpers. A flea can leap thirteen inches in a single jump. That may not seem like much. But fleas are only a fraction of an inch long. If a person could jump that far compared to his or her size, that person would be able to leap over seven hundred feet. The best athletes have only jumped a little over twelve feet. Still, fleas don't get very far by jumping.

18. Which is a synonym for *leap*?

  F walk

  G jump

  H run

  J skip

19. Humans have an advantage over fleas in jumping because humans are

  A much smaller

  B much bigger

  C much quicker

  D much louder

20. How far can a flea leap in a single jump?

  F a fraction of an inch

  G seven hundred feet

  H twelve feet

  J thirteen inches

Although antlers and horns both grow on the heads of animals, they are not the same. They are both made of keratin, the material that fingernails are made of. Horns do not branch. They are attached to the animal's head by a bony core. They grow throughout the animal's life. Cows, goats, and sheep all have horns. Both males and females have them. Antlers branch out and are shed once a year. New antlers grow each year to replace the ones that are shed. Each set of antlers is bigger than the last. Antlers usually grow only on male animals.

21. How are antlers and horns alike?

    A They are shed once a year.

    B They grow throughout the animal's life.

    C They are made of keratin.

    D Each set is bigger than the last.

22. What part of a human body is made of keratin?

    F fingernails

    G antlers

    H horns

    J hair

23. Which animal has antlers?

    A not stated

    B cows

    C goats

    D sheep

When a cartoon character gets hit in the eye, he usually sees stars. This doesn't happen in real life. When people get hit in the eye, they don't see stars, even though they may say they do. What they see is an image of bright light. This image is caused by the nerves in the eye. When the eye is hit, the nerves react by sending signals to the brain. The brain reacts to these signals in the same way that it does when the eye sees a flash of light.

24. What is the main idea of this paragraph?

    F People who get hit in the eye see stars.

    G People who get hit in the eye see light images caused by the eye's nerves.

    H Getting hit in the eye only happens in cartoons.

    J When people are hit in the eye, signals to the brain stop.

25. What happens after the eye is hit?

    A Nerves send signals to the brain.

    B The brain signals the eye to open.

    C People see dark spots.

    D Flashing lights go off.

26. What is a synonym for the word *bright* as it is used in the paragraph?

    F stupid

    G flashing

    H dark

    J intelligent

Some people think the best way to make foods last is to freeze them. Other people store foods in cans. There is yet another, older way to keep food from spoiling. American Indians used heat from the sun to preserve food. They hung meat in the sun to dry it out. When the moisture is gone, germs can't grow and spread. Like other living things, germs need water to stay alive. Today, people don't hang meat in the sun. But they do keep foods like cereal and dried foods in moisture-proof packages.

27. Which sentence does not state a fact?

    A Some people think the best way to make foods last is to freeze them.

    B American Indians used heat from the sun to preserve food.

    C Like other living things, germs need water to stay alive.

    D But they do keep foods like cereal and dried foods in moisture-proof packages.

28. Because foods are dried,

    F they spoil more quickly

    G they are easier to freeze

    H they lack the moisture that allows germs to live

    J they are stored in cans

29. What do germs need to grow and spread?

    A sunlight

    B water

    C cold

    D cereal

"Good morning, madam," said Holmes cheerily. "My name is Sherlock Holmes. Please sit next to the fire. I shall order you a cup of hot coffee. I see that you are shivering."

"It is not cold that makes me shiver," said the woman in a low voice. "It is fear, Mr. Holmes. It is terror." She raised her veil as she spoke. We could see that she was indeed in terrible fear. Her face was tired and gray. She had frightened eyes. Her features were those of a woman of thirty, but her hair was gray.

"You must not fear," he said soothingly. He bent forward to pat her arm. "We shall soon set matters right. I have no doubt."

30. The woman seems to be

    F happy and relaxed

    G worried and afraid

    H quiet and confident

    J angry and sad

31. The writer tells about the woman by describing her

    A thoughts

    B actions

    C home

    D appearance

32. What do you predict Sherlock Holmes will do?

    F Ignore the woman.

    G Call the police.

    H Tell the woman to go home.

    J Help the woman.

Most of the sugar used in cooking and baking comes from the sugar cane plant. Sugar cane grows in the tropics. Before they are harvested, the plants look like bamboo. The stalks are cut when they are about seven feet tall. Piles of the cane are taken to a sugar mill. The stalks are cut and shredded until they are mush. The sweet, liquid part of the mush is called cane juice. The juice is heated until all the water evaporates. What remains are hard, white crystals of sugar.

33. The crystals of sugar are

   A mushy liquids

   B tiny pieces

   C seven feet tall

   D square cubes

34. Where is sugar cane grown?

   F in a sugar mill

   G in the tropics

   H in cool climates

   J not stated

35. What is the meaning of *harvested?*

   A gathered

   B planted

   C watered

   D dried

Pretest Answer Key and Evaluation Chart

This Pretest has been designed to help you determine which reading skills you need to study. This chart shows which skill is being covered with each test question. Circle the questions you answered incorrectly and go to the practice pages in this book covering those skills. Carefully work through all the practice pages before taking the Posttest.

Key

1.	B
2.	H
3.	D
4.	G
5.	C
6.	G
7.	A
8.	F
9.	B
10.	H
11.	D
12.	J
13.	C
14.	F
15.	B
16.	F
17.	B
18.	G
19.	B
20.	J
21.	C
22.	F
23.	A
24.	G
25.	A
26.	G
27.	A
28.	H
29.	B
30.	G
31.	D
32.	J
33.	B
34.	G
35.	A

Tested Skills	Question Numbers	Practice Pages
Synonyms	18, 26	21–24, 25–28
Context clues	35	37–40, 41–44
Spelling	1, 2, 3, 4	45–48, 49–52
Details	20, 22, 34	59–62, 63–66
Sequence	25	67–70, 71–74
Stated concepts	23	75–78, 79–82
Signs	9, 10, 11, 12, 13, 14	89–92
Maps	15, 16, 17	93–96
Graphs	5, 6, 7, 8	97–100, 101–104
Characters	30, 31	119–122, 123–126
Main idea	24	127–130, 131–134
Compare/contrast	21	135–138, 139–142
Drawing conclusions	29	143–146, 147–150, 151–154
Cause and effect	19, 28	155–158, 159–162, 163–166
Predicting outcomes	32	181–184, 185–188
Identifying fact and opinion	27	189–192, 193–196
Applying passage elements	33	197–200, 201–204

Correlation Chart

Correlations Between *Reading Basics* and TABE™ Reading

Reading   Pretest Score _____   Posttest Score _____

Subskill	TABE, Form 7	TABE, Form 8	Practice and Instruction Pages in this Text
6 Words in Context			
same meaning (synonyms)	34	24, 47	21–24, 25–28
opposite meaning (antonyms)		25, 48	29–32, 33–36
appropriate word (context clues)	7, 8, 9, 10, 11, 12, 45	7, 8, 9, 10, 11, 19	37–40, 41–44
spelling	See Test 5 Spelling 1–20	See Test 5 Spelling 1–20	45–48, 49–52
7 Recall Information			
details	19, 22, 24, 47	23, 36, 37, 38	59–62, 63–66
sequence	46	49	67–70, 71–74
stated concepts	1, 2, 18, 50	1, 22, 33	75–78, 79–82
5 Interpret Graphic Information			
signs	3, 4, 5, 6	2, 3, 4, 5, 6	89–92
maps		41, 42, 43, 44, 45	93–96
graphs	30, 31, 32		97–100, 101–104
consumer materials	38, 40, 41, 42	20, 21	105–108, 109–112

Correlation Chart

8 Construct Meaning			
character aspects	36		119–122, 123–126
main idea	43	16, 27, 28, 34	127–130, 131–134
summary/ paraphrase		40	167–170, 171–174
cause/effect	13, 16, 25, 27, 28, 35, 49	30, 46	155–158, 159–162, 163–166
compare/contrast	29	32	135–138, 139–142
conclusion	14, 17, 23, 26, 39, 44	12, 13, 17, 29, 31, 35, 39	143–146, 147–150, 151–154
9 Evaluate/ Extend Meaning			
fact/opinion	20, 33, 48	26	189–192, 193–196
predict outcomes	15, 21, 37	14, 15, 50	181–184, 185–188
apply passage elements		18	197–200, 201–204

Corresponds to TABE™ Forms 7 and 8

Tests of Adult Basic Education are published by CTB Macmillan/McGraw-Hill. Such company has neither endorsed nor authorized this test preparation book.

Words in Context

Understanding Vocabulary

What do you know about words? Look at each of these sports words. Many words we read have a special meaning in a certain context. Write the word under the correct sport.

fly	slam dunk	down	spare	
dribble	home run	split	punt	
out	gutter	huddle	traveling	
jump ball	frame	hike	outfield	

Baseball **Bowling** **Football** **Basketball**

_____ _____ _____ _____

_____ _____ _____ _____

_____ _____ _____ _____

_____ _____ _____ _____

Did you know all the words? Did you use a dictionary? Now choose four of the words. Write a sentence for each word using a meaning that has nothing to do with sports.

_____

_____

_____

_____

_____

Preview Vocabulary

As you read, you may find a word you do not know. There are several things that you can do to learn about the word.

Learning New Words
1. Look at the word and the letters in it.
2. Think of the sounds for the letters.
3. Use the sentence clues that help tell the meaning of the word.
4. Read the word aloud.

Read each of these sentences. Use what you know to figure out the underlined word and its meaning. Write a definition for each underlined word. Use a dictionary if you wish.

1. The very popular actor was surrounded by fans. They <u>besieged</u> him with requests for autographs.

   _____

2. Monica's mother was a <u>chaperon</u> at the dance. She made sure that students obeyed the school rules.

   _____

3. The rain came down hard. Soon the ground was <u>saturated</u> with water.

   _____

4. I had lost interest in mystery stories, but reading an Agatha Christie tale <u>revived</u> my interest in them.

   _____

5. The right lane of the highway was closed, so all the traffic <u>merged</u> into the left lane.

   _____

Recognizing Synonyms

Read the following words: large   big
What do they have in common? They mean about the same thing.
Words that have about the same meanings are called synonyms.

Write the word from the list that is a synonym for the numbered word.

leap	automobile	stroll	pail	sick
intelligent	halt	calm	humorous	talk

1. quiet   _____

2. smart   _____

3. funny   _____

4. jump   _____

5. ill   _____

6. car   _____

7. walk   _____

8. bucket   _____

9. speak   _____

10. stop   _____

Write a synonym for the underlined word in each sentence.

11. The sunset looked <u>pretty</u>. _____

12. Something <u>strange</u> happened at the movie theater. _____

13. People collect many different <u>objects</u>. _____

14. We made a <u>quick</u> trip to the store. _____

15. She <u>inquired</u> about the cost of flights to Florida. _____

16. I put the tomatoes in the <u>sack</u>. _____

17. The girl looked <u>sad</u> about the bad news. _____

18. The <u>smell</u> of flowers filled the air. _____

19. The children rode bicycles down the wide <u>street</u>. _____

20. My friend works in a pet <u>shop</u>. _____

B ▸ Practice

Choose the word that has the meaning closest to that of the underlined word in each sentence.

1. The painting was very underline expensive.

   A costly

   B large

   C cheap

   D exciting

2. The cat crept behind the barn, looking for mice.

   F rushed

   G reached

   H crawled

   J slept

3. The company created a new computer game.

   A sold

   B ruined

   C invented

   D advertised

4. He made an error in the report.

   F statement

   G mistake

   H chart

   J fact

5. The puppies were lively.

   A awake

   B naughty

   C alive

   D active

6. The company had many loyal workers.

   F lazy

   G careful

   H faithful

   J special

7. Wildflowers grew in the meadow.

   A garden

   B field

   C barn

   D window

8. The family moved to a distant city.

   F different

   G new

   H nearby

   J faraway

9. He cheerfully walked along the beach looking for shells.

   A carefully

   B angrily

   C cautiously

   D happily

10. Taking out the trash was her task.

    F chore

    G question

    H garbage

    J problem

C ▶ Apply

Write a new sentence. Use a synonym for each underlined word.

1. We had a <u>nice</u> time at the picnic.

   _____

2. The speaker <u>talked</u> for more than an hour.

   _____

3. I <u>held</u> the kite string tightly.

   _____

4. The artist painted a <u>good</u> picture of the mountains.

   _____

5. Orin did not think the test was <u>hard</u>.

   _____

6. I <u>like</u> to ride roller coasters.

   _____

7. The scary movie had an <u>odd</u> ending.

   _____

8. The family built a new <u>house</u>.

   _____

9. The warm summer weather was <u>pleasant</u>.

   _____

10. The pitcher was <u>upset</u> when the batter hit a home run.

    _____

D Check Up

Replace the underlined word in each sentence with a synonym from the list.

composed	address	famous	noisily	rushed
crowd	gently	normally	aroma	filthy

1. She is <u>usually</u> on time.

_____

2. Van Gogh was a <u>well-known</u> artist.

_____

3. Since I was late, I <u>hurried</u> to the bus stop.

_____

4. The president gave his State of the Union <u>speech</u> last night.

_____

5. The children were <u>dirty</u> after playing in the mud.

_____

6. A huge <u>group</u> of people watched the parade.

_____

7. The <u>smell</u> of the coffee made my mouth water.

_____

8. The children played <u>loudly</u> in the street.

_____

9. She <u>wrote</u> a poem about snow.

_____

Using Synonyms

Heather is very pretty. Everyone agrees that she is beautiful.

In these sentences, *pretty* and *beautiful* mean about the same thing. They are synonyms: different words that have about the same meaning.

When you write, you can use synonyms for variety. You can make your meaning more specific.

Choose the word that is a synonym for each item. Write it on the line.

desk seat lap	**1.** chair _____

plant vase blossom	**2.** flower _____

tale write paragraph	**3.** story _____

friendly awkward formal	**4.** clumsy _____

normal quiet strange	**5.** weird _____

teach build destroy	**6.** instruct _____

varied correct honest	**7.** accurate _____

sadness charity cry	**8.** sorrow _____

magazine article picture	**9.** illustration _____

hardly slowly easily	**10.** simply _____

B Practice

Choose a word from the list that is a synonym for the underlined word in each sentence. Rewrite the sentence using the synonym.

sleepy	clothing	similar	carton	wind
help	relax	locate	untidy	thrill

1. I put the old clothes in a sturdy <u>box</u>.

   _____

2. He would like to <u>rest</u> for an hour after work.

   _____

3. The basement was <u>messy</u> after band practice.

   _____

4. These two stories are <u>alike</u>.

   _____

5. The explorers are trying to <u>find</u> the sunken ship.

   _____

6. The church gave <u>aid</u> to the storm victims.

   _____

7. The circus act will <u>excite</u> the children.

   _____

8. A chilly <u>breeze</u> blew off the ocean.

   _____

9. I always feel <u>drowsy</u> after lunch.

   _____

◆C Apply

Each set of sentences repeats a word. Rewrite the second sentence. Add variety to it by replacing the repeated word with a synonym.

Example: The children put on a program. Everyone enjoyed the program.
Everyone enjoyed the show.

1. The squirrel ran away when the cat came. The squirrel ran away quickly.

   _____

2. She bought some cheap toys at the sale. She gave the cheap things to her dog.

   _____

3. Mario is in a hurry. He is in a big hurry every morning.

   _____

4. Our street is dangerous. There are deep potholes in the street.

   _____

5. The kids laughed at the dog. They always laughed when they played together.

   _____

6. He put his shoes in the bag. Then he put a shirt and some socks into it.

   _____

7. Her ring was shiny. Her pin was shiny too.

   _____

8. They own a small house in the woods. They stay at the house on weekends.

   _____

9. The chef cut the pineapple into pieces. She put the pieces in the salad.

   _____

D Check Up

Circle the answer for each question.

1. She wrote a note to her boss. Which of these words is a synonym for *wrote*?

   A remembered

   B scribbled

   C read

   D sent

2. The children's yelling annoyed her. Which of these words is a synonym for *annoyed*?

   F bothered

   G scared

   H amused

   J helped

3. The settlers struggled to live through the winter. Which of these words is a synonym for *struggled*?

   A hoped

   B had

   C worked

   D wanted

4. The family had a guest staying with them. Which of these words is a synonym for *guest*?

   F party

   G roast

   H visitor

   J belief

5. The pitcher was strong in the ninth inning. Which of these words is **not** a synonym for *strong*?

   A mighty

   B powerful

   C helpful

   D tough

6. Not a sound was heard in the quiet night. Which of these words is **not** a synonym for *quiet*?

   F silent

   G calm

   H peaceful

   J dark

7. The principal was always pleasant when greeting the students. Which of these words is **not** a synonym for *pleasant*?

   A agreeable

   B alert

   C charming

   D nice

8. A customer may complain if the food is not good. Which of these words is **not** a synonym for *complain*?

   F return

   G fuss

   H protest

   J gripe

Recognizing Antonyms

Read the following words: stop   go

Do these words have the same meaning? No, they have opposite meanings. Words with opposite meanings are called *antonyms*. Look for the antonyms in this sentence.

> The hot sun warmed the cold ground.

Hot and *cold* are antonyms.

Find the word in the list that is an antonym for the numbered word. Write the word.

old	happy	finish	first
soft	full	late	big

1. early _____

2. begin _____

3. new _____

4. last _____

5. small _____

6. empty _____

7. sad _____

8. hard _____

Use an antonym for the underlined word to complete the sentence.

9. Yesterday was <u>sunny</u>, but today is _____.

10. I will <u>start</u> the project soon and work until I _____ it.

11. I would rather be <u>first</u> in line than _____.

12. My water bottle is <u>full</u>, but yours is _____.

13. We got up <u>early</u> and worked very _____ into the night.

14. The bed is <u>hard</u>, but the pillow is _____.

15. One clown looked <u>happy</u>; the other looked _____.

B ◆ Practice

Choose an antonym for each word and write the word on the line.

| huge
tiny
large | **1.** gigantic

_____ |
| add
minus
divide | **6.** subtract

_____ |

| long
wide
deep | **2.** short

_____ |
| sleep
run
go | **7.** stop

_____ |

| alike
apart
similar | **3.** together

_____ |
| solution
situation
question | **8.** problem

_____ |

| stay
come
leave | **4.** arrive

_____ |
| every
none
some | **9.** all

_____ |

| alone
same
unusual | **5.** different

_____ |
| small
slender
thick | **10.** thin

_____ |

C ► Apply

Write a sentence using an antonym of the underlined word.

1. Writing my report was <u>challenging</u>.

   _____

2. The <u>huge</u> moth flew to the flower.

   _____

3. I <u>remembered</u> the answer to the test question.

   _____

4. I felt <u>weak</u> when I was exercising.

   _____

5. The actor <u>enters</u> the room through the window.

   _____

6. My dog follows me <u>everywhere</u>.

   _____

7. The animal has a very <u>thick</u> fur coat.

   _____

8. My three friends played tennis <u>with</u> me.

   _____

9. The <u>new</u> store is very near my house.

   _____

10. Two, four, and six are <u>even</u> numbers.

    _____

D ▶ Check Up

Circle the answer for each question.

1. The music was for very young children. Which of these words means the opposite of the word *young?*

   A little

   B old

   C small

   D new

2. The movie came out after the play. Which of these words means the opposite of the word *after?*

   F behind

   G with

   H following

   J before

3. The fastest racers were from France. Which of these words means the opposite of the word *fastest?*

   A quickest

   B biggest

   C slowest

   D nearest

4. We seldom go to a baseball game. Which of these words means the opposite of the word *seldom?*

   F rarely

   G often

   H never

   J soon

5. The stars shown in the night sky. Which of these words means the opposite of the word *night?*

   A noon

   B evening

   C day

   D afternoon

6. The cars parked in the back parking lot. Which of these words means the opposite of the word *back?*

   F side

   G rear

   H front

   J middle

7. We found the keys on the floor of the garage. Which of these words means the opposite of the word *found?*

   A lost

   B gave

   C put

   D stored

8. The drapes were made of dark cloth. Which of these words means the opposite of the word *dark?*

   F purple

   G light

   H short

   J new

A ◆ Introduce

Using Antonyms

The sunny garden was bright. The basement was dark.

In these sentences, *bright* and *dark* have opposite meanings. They are antonyms.

Find the word on the right that is an antonym for each word on the left. Write the word on the line.

1. sleep   _____   end

2. calm   _____   many

3. begin   _____   close

4. filthy   _____   clean

5. few   _____   wake

6. rough   _____   outside

7. open   _____   expensive

8. over   _____   under

9. cheap   _____   excited

10. inside   _____   smooth

B Practice

Read each set of two sentences. On the line, write *antonyms* if the underlined words have opposite meanings. Write *synonyms* if they have the same meaning.

1. The carrots in the salad were <u>raw</u>. The beans were <u>cooked</u>.

   _____

2. The river looked <u>muddy</u>. The bay looked <u>clear</u>.

   _____

3. The boy was <u>rude</u> to his sister. His mom told him to be <u>polite</u>.

   _____

4. The ice was <u>slick</u>. It made the road <u>slippery</u>.

   _____

5. Naomi wore a <u>coarse</u> wool skirt. Her shirt was made of <u>fine</u> silk.

   _____

6. The theater is <u>close</u> to our home. The mall is <u>faraway</u>.

   _____

7. Summers in Canada are <u>mild</u>. Winters are <u>harsh</u>.

   _____

8. I needed a <u>sharp</u> knife to cut the meat. I found a <u>dull</u> knife in the drawer.

   _____

9. The elephant is <u>smart</u>. There are many <u>bright</u> animals at the zoo.

   _____

10. Joe <u>washed</u> the car. He <u>scrubbed</u> off the mud.

   _____

C ▸ Apply

Think of two antonyms to complete each sentence. Write the antonyms on the blanks.

1. The ground was _____ after the rain, but now it is

   _____.

2. The kids _____ a huge sand castle, and then they

   _____ it.

3. The author's first book was _____, but this one is

   _____.

4. I _____ many nice gifts to my family, and I

   _____ some nice ones too.

5. Yesterday the weather was _____, but today it is

   _____.

6. The basketball player is very _____, but his friend is

   _____.

7. It was _____ in the library as people studied but

   _____ in the gym as the crowd cheered.

8. Cars must _____ at red lights and _____ when

   the light turns green.

9. In the tale, the hare was _____, and the tortoise was

   _____.

10. The strawberry tastes _____, and the lemon is

    _____.

D ▶ Check Up

Circle the letter of the word that is an antonym of the underlined word.

1. The dancer moved <u>gracefully</u> across the stage.

   A smoothly

   B nicely

   C clumsily

   D thankfully

2. The march on Washington was <u>peaceful</u>.

   F calm

   G violent

   H whole

   J happy

3. The bread was <u>fresh</u> and delicious.

   A stale

   B homemade

   C sweet

   D new

4. Morris was a very <u>wealthy</u> businessman.

   F evil

   G honest

   H poor

   J lucky

5. The tourists got a <u>friendly</u> welcome.

   A kind

   B unfriendly

   C playful

   D frowning

6. <u>Inside</u> there was a roaring fire.

   F around

   G inn

   H outside

   J indoors

7. Stacy <u>threw</u> the ball quickly.

   A tossed

   B flung

   C hurled

   D caught

8. The room looked <u>gloomy</u> today.

   F scary

   G sad

   H shadowy

   J cheerful

9. The company will <u>increase</u> its work force.

   A add to

   B decrease

   C reward

   D train

10. He was the <u>worst</u> actor for that part.

    F coldest

    G bad

    H best

    J rainiest

Read On Read "A Home in the North." Answer the questions and look for synonyms and antonyms in the article.

A Introduce

Using Context Clues

> The lamp was hideous. It was so ugly that no one bought it.

What does *hideous* mean in this passage? If you do not know the meaning, there are clues to help you. The phrases "so ugly" and "no one bought it" are context clues. They help you figure out that *hideous* means "very ugly."

When you are reading, you may come to a word you do not know. Sometimes you can figure out the meaning of the word from its context. When you figure out a word's meaning from its context, you find other ideas and words around it that give you clues to its meaning.

Synonyms as Context Clues

Sometimes a sentence contains a synonym for a word you do not know. The context of the sentence tells you that the two words are synonyms.

Find the word in each sentence that is a synonym for the underlined word. Write it on the line.

1. The teacher thought a computer was <u>essential</u>, but the students did not think it was necessary.

   Meaning of *essential:* _____

2. The tailor <u>basted</u> the pants before sewing them more carefully.

   Meaning of *basted:* _____

3. She was helpful in a <u>crisis</u>, useful in any kind of emergency.

   Meaning of *crisis:* _____

4. Maria had not <u>intended</u> to leave early. She had planned on staying several hours.

   Meaning of *intended:* _____

B Practice

Antonyms as Context Clues

Sometimes a sentence or passage contains an antonym for a word you do not know. The context tells you that the two words are antonyms. Then you can figure out the meaning of the word you do not know.

Write the word in each sentence that is an antonym for the underlined word. Then write the meaning of the underlined word.

1. Do you like <u>ornate</u> styles or simple ones?

   Antonym of *ornate:* _____

   Meaning of *ornate:* _____

2. William does not like to be <u>idle</u> so he is always active.

   Antonym of *idle:* _____

   Meaning of *idle:* _____

3. The actor used to be <u>humble</u>, but now he acts very proud.

   Antonym of *humble:* _____

   Meaning of *humble:* _____

4. I like bright colors, but my sister likes <u>drab</u> ones.

   Antonym of *drab:* _____

   Meaning of *drab:* _____

5. Although he used to be clumsy, he has become quite <u>agile</u>.

   Antonym of *agile:* _____

   Meaning of *agile:* _____

C Apply

Use context clues to figure out the meaning of each underlined word.
Write the meaning.

1. The fearless soldiers fought bravely.

_____

2. Pat was drowsy on the train, but I was wide awake.

_____

3. Loud music bothered him, and barking dogs irked him even more.

_____

4. Many people helped construct the bridge, which was built in the early 1900s.

_____

5. Anton enrolled in English classes and also signed up for computer lessons.

_____

6. Until the typhoon struck, the sailors had never seen such a bad storm at sea.

_____

7. He was glum, and his friends did not know why he was so sad.

_____

8. It was a bad blunder, but the coach excused the mistake.

_____

9. The farmers exported some of their corn, sending it to other countries.

_____

10. It was warm and sunny; in fact, the weather was balmy.

_____

Read each passage. Then answer the vocabulary question that follows. Use context clues to help you answer the questions.

1. The first ballpoint pens were awful. They were about as neat and accurate as crayons. Sometimes the ink would swell up in the pen. Then the pen would burst. The ink took a long time to dry on the page. It would sometimes smear all over the page. Then the words were impossible to read.

   To be *accurate* is to be

   A exact and tidy

   B sloppy and messy

   C rushed

   D hard to read

2. The first humans in North America got there by walking. They crossed the Bering Sea from Asia. The sea was frozen. They came during the Great Ice Age. Scientists think it was about twenty-five thousand years ago. The precise date is not known.

   Another word for *precise* is

   F long-ago

   G simple

   H exact

   J month

3. One of the largest waterfalls in the world makes no noise. It also does not move. The Petrified Waterfall looks like a cascade frozen in time. It is found in Turkey. But the falls aren't ice; they have turned to stone.

   As used in the passage, *cascade* means

   A forest

   B waterfall

   C quiet

   D a long period of time

4. Trees have a vertical shape, instead of a long, low one. They grow upward. We don't ask why. But they do so for a good reason. They are reaching for the sun. Sunlight gives trees energy.

   Something that is *vertical* is

   F running sideways

   G growing all around

   H very short

   J standing straight up and down

Using Context Clues

The farmer used a reaper, a big machine that cuts grain. You may not know what a *reaper* is. But you know the meaning of *reaper* after you read the sentence above. The sentence includes a group of words that defines *reaper*. It tells you that a reaper is a big machine that cuts grain.

Read the sentences. Use the context clues to figure out the meaning of each underlined word. Then write the meaning of each word.

1. The boss said I have <u>gumption</u>, or common sense.

   _____

2. People in India are born into <u>castes</u>, or social groups.

   _____

3. Peanuts are <u>legumes</u>, plants in the bean family.

   _____

4. In the greenhouse we saw an <u>orchid</u>, a valuable flower from the rain forest.

   _____

5. Birds have a <u>gizzard</u>, a body part that grinds up food.

   _____

6. The golfer took several <u>strokes</u>, or swings of the club, to hit the ball.

   _____

7. Some birds grab fish with their <u>talons</u>, or claws.

   _____

8. Scientists can make <u>synthetic</u>, or man-made, fuels.

   _____

B ▸ Practice

Read each sentence. Write the word or words that give context clues to the meaning of the underlined word. Some are synonyms. Some are antonyms. Some are groups of words that describe the word.

1. Miguel wanted a <u>yacht</u>, but he bought a smaller boat.

   _____

2. I <u>loathe</u> spiders, and I hate snakes too.

   _____

3. Mom tried to <u>console</u> the baby, but she could not comfort her.

   _____

4. Kwon said he was healthy, but he did not seem <u>robust</u>.

   _____

5. We saw a <u>spring peeper</u>, a kind of tree frog.

   _____

6. Mr. Green told me to <u>modify</u>, or change, the plan.

   _____

7. Sometimes Mr. Ivy is rude, but today he is very <u>polite</u>.

   _____

8. Ads use many <u>gimmicks</u>, or tricks, to sell things.

   _____

9. Should we <u>expose</u> the facts or hide them?

   _____

10. There was a <u>blizzard</u>, a big snowstorm, last winter.

    _____

C ▸ Apply

Use context clues to figure out the meaning of each underlined word. Write the meaning.

1. The plant looks <u>fragile</u>, but it is very strong.

   _____

2. Will they <u>forbid</u> the trip or permit you to go?

   _____

3. My shirt was <u>immaculate</u> this morning, but now it is dirty.

   _____

4. <u>Jaguars</u>, large cats from the South American jungle, are good hunters.

   _____

5. There was a lot of <u>amusement</u> at the party, but I was not having fun.

   _____

6. During the Ice Age, some animals <u>adapted</u>, or got used to, the cold.

   _____

7. He lives like a <u>hermit</u>, never seeing other people.

   _____

8. The water is kept in a <u>reservoir</u>, a man-made lake.

   _____

9. He <u>crumpled</u>, or crushed, the paper.

   _____

10. Being in the flood was an <u>ordeal</u>, a very hard experience.

   _____

Read each passage. Then circle the answer for each question.

1. Roots are an important part of a plant. Roots are usually hidden under the ground. Some float free in water. Some get water from the air. They all do the same job. They bring <u>nutrition</u>, food and water, to the plant.

   Nutrition is

   A air

   B food

   C roots

   D a plant

2. A zebra might hide in tall grass. It travels in a big herd. It has to look out for tigers. They eat zebras. It has to look out for lions too. The zebra is the <u>prey</u> of more than one animal.

   An animal that is *prey* is

   F tall

   G hunted by other animals for food

   H a deadly fighter

   J tame

3. The sand lizard is not big and strong, but it can do many things. It is fast. It can dig tunnels through sand dunes. It dives into the sand and <u>burrows</u> with its back legs.

   When the lizard *burrows*, it

   A digs

   B runs

   C slides

   D shouts for help

4. Jungle animals are not like animals that live in open spaces. They don't need <u>keen</u> eyesight to see far away. They don't need a good sense of smell, either. Instead, jungle animals rely on their ears.

   Eyesight that is *keen* is

   F sharp

   G wide

   H long

   J blurred

Read On Read "What Is Color?" Answer the questions and use context clues as you read the article.

Spelling Words

Spelling words correctly is an important part of writing. You can improve your spelling by learning a few rules and by working on a few common problems.

Homophones

Homophones are words that sound the same. They are spelled differently and have different meanings.

> Your friends are <u>here</u>. Can you <u>hear</u> that music?

The words *here* and *hear* sound the same. But they have different meanings and different spellings.

Adding Suffixes to Words with Silent *e* and Final *y*

Many words have a silent *e* at the end. When you add endings such as *-ing, -y,* or *-ion*, the *e* is usually dropped.

> I can <u>make</u> a cake. I am <u>making</u> a birthday cake for Rob.

Some words, like *carry*, end in a consonant and *y*. When an ending such as *-s, -est, -ed,* or *-ly* is added to a word like this, the *y* is usually changed to *i*.

> I can <u>carry</u> my bag. I <u>carried</u> my bag through the airport.

Words with Silent Letters

Some words have letters that are not pronounced. For example, in *comb*, the *b* is not pronounced. Work on remembering the silent letters in *comb* and other words with silent letters: *wrap, know, lamb.*

B Practice

Read each sentence. Then write the underlined word with a new ending for the second sentence. Choose from the endings -s, -d, -ed, -y, or -ing. Be sure to spell the word correctly when adding the ending.

1. Did the baby <u>cry</u> during the night?

   The baby _____ until he went to sleep.

2. Do you like the <u>taste</u> of carrots?

   Carrots make a _____ cake.

3. They decided to <u>marry</u> in June.

   They were _____ yesterday.

4. Don't <u>tire</u> yourself on the long walk.

   A hike through the woods can be _____.

5. The cat likes to <u>hide</u> from the family.

   The cat is _____ under the bed.

6. The batter will <u>try</u> to get to base.

   Last inning the batter _____ to hit a home run.

7. James must <u>hurry</u> every morning.

   Yesterday James _____ to catch the bus.

8. Should we <u>drive</u> to the Grand Canyon?

   My family loves _____ to distant places.

9. She made a <u>cherry</u> pie.

   The _____ were from the tree in the yard.

10. <u>State</u> your opinion in your speech.

    Ana is good at _____ her opinion.

C ▸ Apply

Write the word from the list that completes each sentence. Underline the silent letter in each word.

hour	sign	knee	climb	wrong

1. The store had a big _____ in the window.

2. The caller dialed a _____ number.

3. Would you like to _____ to the top of a mountain?

4. We waited for an _____ for the doctor.

5. He hurt his _____ when he jumped over the fence.

Write the homophone from the list that correctly completes each sentence.

by	road	right	through	weak
buy	rode	write	threw	week

6. I went to the music store to _____ a CD.

7. The baby was too _____ to sit up.

8. Turn _____ at the next street.

9. The campers _____ horses every morning.

10. You will enjoy your walk _____ the forest.

◤D◢ Check Up

Read the passages below. Then write each numbered word. If the word is misspelled, spell it correctly. If it is correct, write it as it is.

(1) Coud you eat with your head upside down? Flamingos always eat that way. Flamingos look like pink swans. They have long, thin legs. They like (2) liveing near the (3) see or large lakes. They have bright red to (4) pail pink feathers.

A flamingo has a large bill. The top (5) haf of the bill is like a scoop. To eat, the flamingo turns its head over. It dips its bill into the water. With (6) its comb, it can be seen (7) rakeing (8) threw the mud for small animals.

1. _____   5. _____

2. _____   6. _____

3. _____   7. _____

4. _____   8. _____

Most insects are not good mothers. They have the habit of laying (1) there eggs and (2) leaveing them. They are not good at (3) careing for (4) their young. But the earwig is different. A earwig acts like a (5) loveing mother. She stays with the eggs. She cleans them. When they are hatched, she can be seen (6) taking the (7) babies for food. Earwig (8) familys stay together. This is unusual for insects.

1. _____   5. _____

2. _____   6. _____

3. _____   7. _____

4. _____   8. _____

Spelling Words: Words with *ei* and *ie*

Words spelled with the vowel combinations *ei* and *ie* can be confusing.

> Can you <u>believe</u> that?
>
> Did you <u>receive</u> the gift?

Both these words have a long *e* vowel sound. The rule "*i* before *e* except after *c*" can help you spell them.
In some words, *ei* has a long *a* vowel sound.

> <u>Eight neighbors</u> came over for a picnic.

Doubling the Final Consonant and Changing *f* to *v*

> Don't <u>slip</u> on the wet <u>leaf</u>.
>
> She <u>slipped</u> on the wet <u>leaves</u>.

Some one-syllable words, like *slip*, have a short vowel and end in one consonant. Before adding the endings *-ed, -ing, -er,* and *-est,* you should double the final consonant.
In some words, like *leaf* and *life*, the final *f* or *fe* changes to *v* when endings are added.

Write *ie* or *ei* in each blank to correctly spell the word.

1. A th_____f took the woman's ring and watch.

2. A spider web hung from the c_____ling.

3. Oil is the ch_____f product of that country.

4. How much does the baby w_____gh?

5. The cool rain was a great rel_____f.

6. The horses pulled a sl_____gh over the snow.

7. Everyone ate a p_____ce of cake.

8. The farmer planted corn in the f_____ld.

B Practice

Read each sentence. Then write the underlined word with a new ending for the second sentence. Use the endings *-ed, -ing, -y, -er,* or *-est*. Be sure to change the spelling correctly for the new ending.

1. She has a <u>plan</u> for a new kitchen.

   She is _____ to buy a new stove.

2. Take care not to <u>rip</u> your sweater.

   Chris _____ his sweater in the soccer game.

3. Stacy likes to <u>shop</u> for clothes.

   Stacy goes _____ almost every weekend.

4. The coach likes to have <u>fun</u> at practice.

   He tells some _____ jokes.

5. Toby has always been <u>slim</u>.

   She is _____ than ever.

6. Do you want to <u>grab</u> lunch?

   Yesterday we _____ lunch at the pizza place.

7. Chad can <u>dig</u> with a shovel.

   He is _____ a fish pond in his yard.

8. Woodpeckers <u>tap</u> on tree trunks.

   They have been _____ all morning.

9. The <u>sun</u> might shine today.

   It has not been _____ for a week.

10. You can put fresh tomatoes in a <u>can</u>.

    Last summer we _____ a bushel of tomatoes.

C Apply

Read each sentence. Write a new sentence with the underlined word. Make the underlined word plural. Remember to make spelling changes for the new ending.

1. A <u>wolf</u> howled all night.

_____

2. I made a <u>loaf</u> of banana bread.

_____

3. He dressed as an <u>elf</u> for the holiday party.

_____

4. A <u>thief</u> took the money out of the car.

_____

5. Make <u>yourself</u> a cup of tea.

_____

6. The <u>shelf</u> held many books.

_____

7. The <u>life</u> of a mountain climber is risky.

_____

8. The florist took a <u>leaf</u> off the stem.

_____

9. The butter <u>knife</u> is dirty.

_____

10. She wore a <u>scarf</u> on her head.

_____

◆ D ▶ Check Up

Read the paragraphs below. Then write each numbered word. If the word is misspelled, spell it correctly. If it is correct, write it as it is written.

Healthy kittens make (1) grate pets. (2) Their are ways to tell if a kitten is healthy. (3) It's eyes should be clear. The kitten (4) shoud not have fleas or other bugs. A healthy kitten has a full, glossy coat, with no (5) bear patches. It is not (6) to fat or (7) skiny. It has white teeth and pink gums. And it doesn't have a (8) dripy nose. All these (9) sines tell (10) weather or not a kitten is healthy.

1. _____   6. _____

2. _____   7. _____

3. _____   8. _____

4. _____   9. _____

5. _____   10. _____

(1) Write now, (2) your standing on a (3) moveing rock. You (4) sea, the earth's crust is not solid. It is (5) maid up of huge plates of rock. Some of the plates are (6) biger than the continents. (7) There always shifting because of forces within the earth. Some scientists (8) beleive that the (9) great heat inside the earth causes the movement. The inside of the planet is thousands of degrees (10) hoter than the surface.

1. _____   6. _____

2. _____   7. _____

3. _____   8. _____

4. _____   9. _____

5. _____   10. _____

 **Read On** Read "Who Wears the Pants?" Answer the questions and study the spelling of words in the article.

Review

Synonyms

Words that have about the same meanings are called *synonyms*.

The boy was *scared* of snakes and *frightened* by spiders.

Antonyms

Words with opposite meanings are called *antonyms*.

Some plants like *sun;* other plants like *shade*.

Context Clues

You can figure out the meaning of a word by using other ideas and words around it.

The farmer looked at his *wilted* crops. If it did not rain soon, the crops would die.

Spelling Words

Some words sound the same but are spelled differently.

eight   ate

Some words have silent letters.
knew   wrinkle   thumb

Some words change their spelling when endings are added.

rake—raking   wolf—wolves

Some words double the final consonant when endings are added.

clap—clapped   grab—grabbed

Some words have unusual spellings.

receive   weigh

Assessment

Read the paragraphs and circle the answer for each question.

Underground tunnels for cars and trains are <u>common</u>. But in England there is an underground tunnel for boats. Owners of a coal mine built this canal. They save money by <u>transporting</u> coal underground. Coal is loaded into the boats. Then workers lie on their backs on top of the coal. They push against the roof of the tunnel with their feet to move the boats.

1. Which word is an antonym for *common?*

   A silly

   B ordinary

   C popular

   D unusual

2. The word *transporting* means

   F changing something from one language to another

   G carrying something from one place to another

   H replanting something in another place

   J changing the appearance of something

   Some people are afraid of flying. They hear about plane crashes. They worry about their own safety. <u>Experts</u> say it is more <u>dangerous</u> to travel in a car. Many more people die in car crashes than in plane crashes. These highly skilled and knowledgeable people have testified that airplanes are really quite safe.

3. Another word for *dangerous* is

   A exciting

   B boring

   C risky

   D routine

4. An *expert* is a

   F newspaper reporter

   G college student

   H Supreme Court judge

   J highly skilled and knowledgeable person

Many people like the tart taste of lemon on fish. But lemon was added to cooked fish for another reason. People in the Middle Ages thought that lemon juice could dissolve bones. People could then eat fish without the fear of choking on the bones.

5. Which word is an antonym for *tart?*

    A sweet

    B sour

    C hot

    D salty

6. The word *dissolve* means

    F to divide into portions

    G to twist out of shape

    H to go in different directions

    J to cause to disappear

    Floods can be very destructive. They can cause severe damage to homes. But floods aren't always dreaded, and some are good for the land. In Ancient Egypt, floods were helpful. Egypt is a flat, dry country. Each year, the Nile River rose over its banks and water covered all the nearby land. The flooding washed new, fertile soil over the land. As a result, Ancient Egypt had great farmland.

7. Which word in the paragraph is an antonym for *destructive?*

    A severe

    B helpful

    C dry

    D new

8. Fertile soil

    F is full of rocks

    G does not absorb water

    H is able to produce good crops

    J is not used for farming

Circle the word that is spelled correctly and best completes each sentence.

9. The department store is having its annual summer _____.

   A sail

   B sale

   C sal

   D sael

10. My grandparents were _____ right after World War II.

    F marryed

    G marryied

    H maried

    J married

11. The _____ bulb in the closet was burned out.

    A liegt

    B lihgt

    C light

    D liet

12. Our dentist is also our new _____.

    F naybor

    G neighbor

    H nieghbor

    J naighbor

13. I am _____ a trip to California.

    A takking

    B takeing

    C taking

    D taeking

14. The clerk gave her a _____ for her purchase.

    F receipt

    G reciept

    H receight

    J reicept

15. The farmer put the _____ out in the pasture.

    A calfs

    B calfes

    C calves

    D calvs

16. The doctor put a cast on the patient's broken _____.

    F rist

    G wrist

    H wist

    J whrist

17. Did the dog _____ his bone in the yard?

    A bery

    B beary

    C bury

    D barey

18. A sharp _____ is easier to use than a dull one.

    F nife

    G knive

    H kniefe

    J knife

Recalling Information

Detailed Information

Every day you follow directions—at home, in school, or in the workplace. When you read directions, you pay attention to details and follow the steps in the order they are given. Read and follow the directions.

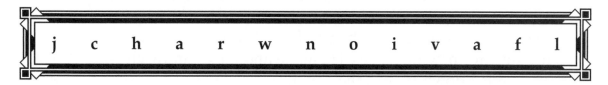

j c h a r w n o i v a f l

1. Draw a box around the letter **o**.

2. Underline the letter **h**.

3. Cross out the letter **j**.

4. Draw a circle around the letter **f**.

5. Put a check mark on top of the letter **w**.

6. Write the word that is left. _____

Write directions on how to draw something. Follow your own directions on a separate sheet of paper. Then give your directions to a friend to follow. How does his or her picture compare to yours?

Use these words if you wish: *wavy, slanted, straight, circle, under, square.*

1. _____
2. _____
3. _____
4. _____
5. _____
6. _____
7. _____

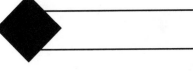

What Comes Next?

Sequence words tell the order of events. Some sequence words are *first, next, last, today,* and *yesterday*. It is important to know the sequence when telling or reading a story.

Frank came home from work. Before he took off his coat and hung it up, he brought the mail in from the mailbox. Then he went into the kitchen and checked the answering machine for new messages. He made and ate a sandwich and settled down to read the paper.

1. What did Frank do first after he came home?   _____

2. What did Frank do next?   _____

3. What did Frank do before he made a sandwich?   _____

4. What did Frank do last?   _____

Number the following words to show the correct time order.

_____ last Sunday   _____ tonight   _____ tomorrow

_____ today   _____ next Tuesday   _____ yesterday

Use sequence words to write about something that happened to you in the last week.

_____

_____

_____

_____

_____

_____

A ◆ Introduce

Recognizing Details

When you read, it is important to pay attention to details. They help you understand what you are reading. They also help you figure out the main idea.

Read the passage below. Then choose the correct answer for each question.

Would you rather climb a mountain or travel from one country to another? There's one place where you can do both at the same time. It's Mont Blanc. Mont Blanc is a mountain in the Alps. Its name means "white mountain" in French. Its peak is the highest point in the mountain range. Mont Blanc lies along the border between France and Italy. The border divides the mountain almost exactly in half. The peak, however, is in France.

1. Mont Blanc is
   A a country
   B a mountain range
   C a mountain
   D a glacier

2. Mont Blanc lies between
   F the Alps and France
   G France and Switzerland
   H northern and southern Italy
   J France and Italy

3. In which country is the peak of the mountain located?
   A Italy
   B France
   C the Alps
   D the border

4. The mountain's name means
   F "on the border"
   G "highest point"
   H "white mountain"
   J "two countries"

Read each passage. Write the detail that answers each question.

Bees don't sting unless they have to. They only sting to defend themselves. Worker bees have only one stinger. They can only sting once. They leave their stingers behind when they sting a person or an animal. The stinger keeps pumping poison into the wound. But the bee dies a few hours later. Drones, the male bees, don't have any stingers.

1. For what reason do bees sting?

_____

2. What happens to a worker bee after it stings a person or an animal?

_____

3. What kind of bees have no stingers?

_____

There are two countries where men wear skirts from time to time. The skirts are traditional costumes. The skirts worn in Scotland are known as kilts. Each Scottish family, or clan, has its own special plaid pattern and colors. The guards outside the Greek parliament building also wear kilts. Theirs are white. This is also an old, respected tradition.

4. In what two countries do men sometimes wear skirts?

_____

5. What are the skirts worn by men called?

_____

6. In Greece, who are the men who wear kilts?

_____

Details support the main idea of a paragraph. Read each paragraph. Write four details that support its main idea.

Ducks are well suited to their environment. Their bodies are built for swimming and fishing. Ducks have short wings so they can dive underwater. They have long necks for catching food. Their webbed feet make good paddles for swimming. And although ducks live in water, they don't get very wet. They have a gland under their tails that gives off a waxy oil. Ducks rub this oil over their feathers with their bills. Water rolls off a duck's waterproof feathers.

Main Idea: Ducks are well suited to their environment.
Details:

1. _____

2. _____

3. _____

4. _____

Pilgrim churches had many strict rules. Older men sat on one side of the church and young men sat on the other. Boys could not sit near girls. Most of the boys sat on the stairs. There was a special guard to make sure that children didn't talk. He also kept an eye on those who seemed to be falling asleep. He carried a long rod to prod children who weren't paying attention.

Main Idea: Pilgrim churches had many strict rules.
Details:

5. _____

6. _____

7. _____

8. _____

◆D◆ Check Up

Read the passage below. Then choose the correct answer for each question.

Firefighters use crowbars to open stuck doors. Builders may use crowbars to pry up shingles or floorboards. Do you know why this tool is named after a bird? It has to do with its shape. A crowbar is an iron bar. It is about two feet long. It is about an inch thick. The bar's shape makes it a good lever. One end is curved like a fishhook. The other end is flat. It has a sharp edge that looks like a wedge. To some people, the shape looked like the beak of a crow. They called the whole thing a crowbar.

1. According to the passage, firefighters use crowbars to

   A put out fires

   B pull up floorboards

   C open doors

   D remove shingles

2. The crowbar's name comes from

   F an iron bar

   G a fishhook

   H a tool

   J a bird

3. A crowbar is made of

   A steel

   B shingles

   C iron

   D wood

4. The size of a crowbar is

   F a foot long and two inches thick

   G two feet long and an inch thick

   H a foot long and one inch thick

   J two feet long and two inches thick

5. A crowbar is used as

   A a wrench

   B an inclined plane

   C a lever

   D a pulley

6. One end of a crowbar looks like

   F the beak of a crow

   G a lever

   H a large fish

   J shingles or floorboards

 **Introduce**

Recalling Details

Details are specific facts. They support the main idea of a passage. They help you enjoy reading the passage. They help you understand the main idea.

Read the passage. Then circle the answer for each question.

There is plenty of life on the seashore. Ocean water collects in little pools between the rocks. These are sometimes called rock pools. The pools are safe from waves. They are warmer than the ocean. Sea animals live in the pools. Hermit crabs live there. They live in the old shells of other animals. There are lots of empty shells in the pools. Starfish live there too. They do well in the calm water.

1. What is the name of the little pools near the ocean?

    A seashore

    B hermit crabs

    C rock pools

    D safe pools

2. What is one reason sea animals live in the pools?

    F The water is warmer than in the ocean.

    G There are lots of waves.

    H The water is icy.

    J The rocks are dry.

3. What do hermit crabs find in the pools that help them live?

    A starfish

    B rocks

    C waves

    D old shells

B ▶ Practice

Read the passages. Then answer the questions.

The World's Fair was held in New York City in 1964. Many amazing things were shown there. One was the world's largest piece of cheese. It was a huge chunk of cheddar. The cheese weighed more than thirty-four thousand pounds. It was brought from Wisconsin. That state is famous for its cheese. The cheese was too big for a car or plane. It was carried to the fair on a huge trailer. This was called the "Cheese-Mobile."

Write two details from the passage about the World's Fair.

1. _____

2. _____

Write two details about the big piece of cheese.

3. _____

4. _____

The human tongue can taste four flavors. These are sweet, sour, salty, and bitter. Tongues have taste buds. They are on the front, sides, and back of the tongue. Taste buds react to chemicals in food. They send signals to the brain. The brain sorts out the signals.

Write two details about the human tongue.

5. _____

6. _____

Write two details about taste buds.

7. _____

8. _____

C Apply

Read the passages. Then answer the questions.

Sloths are almost always upside down. They live and walk upside down. Sloths live in rain forests in Brazil. They hang from tree branches by using their long, curved claws. They eat leaves, buds, and twigs. They are so quiet that moss grows in their hair. They move very slowly. Moving so slowly helps sloths blend in with the trees. Then they aren't seen and caught by other animals.

1. Where do sloths live?

   _____

2. What do sloths eat?

   _____

3. What do sloths use to hang from tree branches?

   _____

The Dutch call their wooden shoes *klompen*. That word sounds like the noise the shoe makes. Why would they wear such noisy shoes? The land in Holland is below sea level. The land is very wet. So, long ago the Dutch people made shoes out of wood. The shoes kept their feet dry. But they were noisy. They were not easy to wear. Few Dutch people wear them anymore.

4. What do the Dutch call their wooden shoes?

   _____

5. In what country do the Dutch people live?

   _____

6. What is unusual about the land in Holland?

   _____

7. Why did the Dutch people wear wooden shoes?

   _____

Read the passage. Then circle the answer for each question.

Many people in India live in mud houses. These people are so poor that they can't afford to build any other kind of house. Mud doesn't cost anything. The people take wet mud and pack it together. They make mud blocks and leave them to dry in the sun. The dried mud makes strong bricks. The people tie the mud blocks together with straw. They build their homes with these blocks. In many parts of India, whole villages are made of mud.

1. According to this passage, in what country do people build mud houses?

   A United States

   B Israel

   C India

   D Ireland

2. What is the main reason people use mud for houses?

   F Mud is attractive.

   G Mud keeps houses warm.

   H Mud is easy to build with.

   J Mud is free.

3. People use mud for houses by

   A making blocks out of it

   B shaping wet mud into walls

   C putting it between blocks

   D building a dirt house and putting water on the dirt

4. How do people dry the mud blocks?

   F in the rain

   G in the sun

   H in a well

   J in an oven

5. What material besides mud is used for mud houses in India?

   A bricks

   B straw

   C clay

   D cement blocks

6. If you are traveling in India, you may see

   F brick houses

   G straw houses

   H wealthy villages

   J mud villages

Read On   Read "Egypt's Wonders." Answer the questions and look for details in the article.

A ▶ Introduce

Identifying Sequence

One way writers tell when events happen in a story is by using time order. They write the steps in the order in which they occur, starting with the first step. Another way writers tell when events happen is by using words such as *first, then, next, before, after,* and *finally.*

Read the passage. Then choose the correct answer to each question.

When Stanley Willoughby was eight years old, he was run over by a steamroller. Believe it or not, he lived to tell the tale. In 1951, the young boy saw a huge iron machine pressing new tar on his street. He soon walked up behind the roller to get a better look. But then the machine went into reverse. The driver heard Stanley's screams and stopped quickly. He jumped out of his seat and found the boy on the street. Stanley's legs had been run over, but they weren't crushed. The roller had pressed his body into the fresh, soft asphalt. If the street had been hard, poor Stanley would have been crushed.

1. What happened right before the steamroller went into reverse?

   A The driver heard Stanley's screams.

   B Stanley lay in the street.

   C Stanley walked up to look at the roller.

   D The driver stopped the roller.

2. What did the driver do right after Stanley screamed?

   F put the steamroller in reverse

   G helped the boy on the street

   H stopped the steamroller

   J continued backing up

3. What phrase tells when the entire sequence of events happened?

   A believe it or not

   B in 1951

   C soon

   D but then

Read each passage. Then write the steps of what happens in order.

The ancient Romans built more than 93,500 miles of roads. The first step in building a road was to dig down until firm soil was reached. The bottom layer of sand and lime was laid on that firm soil. On top of that, four more layers were placed. One was made of stones that were held together with clay and cement. The next layer served as waterproofing. Then a layer made of lime, sand, earth, and brick was put down. On top was the smooth surface of the road.

Steps: Building a Roman Road

1. Dig down until firm soil is reached.

2. _____

3. _____

4. _____

5. _____

A cowhand's horse was his most important tool. Cow ponies were half wild mustang and half Eastern workhorse. They roamed free until the age of four. They lived on wild grass. Then in late spring the cowhands would corral the wild ponies. Next they would send the ponies to special trainers called bronco busters. Bronco busters would put the ponies through a rough training called "breaking" or "busting." Finally, cowhands would use the ponies to round up cattle.

Steps: The Life of a Cow Pony

1. Ponies roamed free until the age of four.

2. _____

3. _____

4. _____

5. _____

C ▸ Apply

Read each passage. Then answer the questions.

Dust devils are a type of whirlwind. They appear in deserts all over the world. They are spinning columns of air. They get started on hot, dry days. First the sand gets very hot from the sun. It gets hot faster than the air above it does. Because heat rises, the air near the ground may rush upward. This rush of air pulls more air behind it. Air currents wrap around the rising air and spin around it. The whirlwind has a cone shape. In the end, it spins across the desert.

1. What is the first thing that happens when a dust devil forms?

_____

2. What happens after desert sand gets very hot?

_____

3. How does a lot of air get pulled upward?

_____

4. What is the last thing that happens to a dust devil before it starts spinning across the desert?

_____

5. What does a dust devil do after it has been formed?

_____

D▶ Check Up

Read each passage. After each passage, the steps described in it are listed in incorrect order. Number the steps to show the correct order of the events.

Bob Hail was happy to find out he'd broken his nose. Why? He was in an accident that could have killed him. In 1972, Hail was learning to skydive. Soon his turn came, and he jumped from the plane along with the other students. But when he was in the air, he realized he had no parachute. He didn't have a backup chute either. He dropped more than three thousand feet. He reached a speed of eighty miles an hour. Without a parachute, there was nothing to slow his fall. When he hit the ground, he landed on his face. In the end, Hail walked away from the crash with just a broken nose and a few missing teeth.

_____ Bob dropped more than three thousand feet.

_____ Bob jumped from the plane.

_____ Bob realized he didn't have a parachute.

_____ Bob landed on the ground on his face.

Ancient Greek myths say that the first echo was a beautiful young maiden. Echo had only one fault. She talked too much. One of the Greek gods was angered by her constant talking, so he cast a spell on her. After that Echo could never speak on her own. All she could do was repeat the last words of others. Then Echo fell in love with a handsome young man. His name was Narcissus. But the young man did not love Echo. He loved only himself. Echo became so sad that she faded away, until all that was left of her was her voice.

_____ Echo fell in love with Narcissus.

_____ A Greek god cast a spell to keep Echo from speaking on her own.

_____ Echo faded away, until only her voice was left.

_____ Echo talked too much.

Recognizing Sequence

When you read a story, you don't notice only *what* happens. You notice *when* the events happen. Often you need to know that one thing happened before or after another.

When you read, look for words that show the order of events, such as *first, next, then, later,* and *finally.* They will help you understand when things happen. They will also help you remember the order of events.

Read the passage. Then circle the answer to each question.

Butter is made from the fat in cream. When cream is shaken, the fat comes together. It forms bits of butter. After the bits have formed, a liquid is left. This is called buttermilk. The buttermilk is drained off. Next, the butter bits are washed with cold water. Then they are drained and salted. In the final stage, the butter is mixed well.

1. What is the first step in making butter?

   A Drain the liquid.

   B Wash the butter bits.

   C Shake the cream.

   D Salt the butter.

2. What happens right after the butter bits are formed?

   F They are washed with cold water.

   G The buttermilk is poured off.

   H They are mixed well.

   J The fat comes together.

3. Which word is **not** used to signal when a step happens?

   A after

   B next

   C because

   D then

4. What is the last step in making butter?

   F mixing

   G shaking

   H draining

   J salting

Read the passages. After the passages, the steps are described. They are in incorrect order. Write the correct order of the steps.

Maple syrup is made from the sap of maple trees. In the late winter, farmers tap maple trees. First they bore a three-inch hole in the tree trunk. The hole is about four feet off the ground. Then they put a metal or wooden spout in the hole. They hang a bucket from the spout. Sap drips out of the spout. It goes into the bucket. Once a day the farmers collect the sap. They boil it. The water boils away. Maple syrup is left.

Correct order of steps:

A The farmers boil the sap.   _____

B The farmers put a hole in the tree.   _____

C Sap drips from the spout.   _____

D The farmers put a spout in the hole.   _____

E The farmers hang a bucket from the tree.   _____

In 1863, the first subway was opened. It was built in London, England. The first step was to dig up the road by the stations. A deep ditch was dug. Then tracks were laid in the ditch. Next, brick arches were built over the tracks. Finally, a new road was laid on top of the arches.

Correct order of steps:

A Tracks were laid in the ditch.   _____

B The road was dug up.   _____

C A new road was laid on top.   _____

D A deep ditch was dug.   _____

E Brick arches were built over the tracks.   _____

C Apply

Read the passage. Then answer the questions.

In A.D. 1014, England was ruled by King Ethelred. The city of London was attacked by fierce Danes. King Ethelred had to flee. A Norse named Olaf brought his ships to London to help the king. But he could not get near the city. The Danes held London Bridge. So Olaf tied ropes to the stakes that held the bridge up. He attached the other ends to his ships. Then his men rowed as hard as they could. The stakes were pulled out. The bridge came crashing down. Olaf then conquered the city. King Ethelred returned to the throne.

1. Why did King Ethelred have to leave London?

   _____

2. Why did Olaf bring ships to London?

   _____

3. What did Olaf do after he could not get across London Bridge?

   _____

4. What did Olaf's men do after Olaf tied his ships to the bridge stakes?

   _____

5. What was the final result of Olaf's action?

   _____

D ▶ Check Up

Read the passage. Then circle the answer for each question.

The Hope diamond is the largest blue diamond in the world. It is worth a lot of money. People say that a curse haunts the owner of the gem. Five hundred years ago, a Hindu priest stole it from a temple statue. He was killed for the crime. Later, a Frenchman owned the diamond. He was killed by wild dogs. Then the French royal family got the Hope diamond. One of the princesses was killed by a mob. Marie Antoinette, the queen, was beheaded. The next owner was Jacques Celot. He killed himself. Later Thomas Henry Hope bought the diamond. He had no bad luck. The diamond was finally bought by the Smithsonian Institution in Washington, D.C.

1. When does the history of the Hope diamond begin?

    A during the French revolution

    B the 20th century

    C five hundred years ago

    D five years ago

2. Who was the first owner of the Hope diamond?

    F the French royal family

    G Jacques Celot

    H Thomas Henry Hope

    J a Hindu priest

3. Who owned the diamond before the French royal family?

    A Jacques Celot

    B a Frenchman who was killed by wild dogs

    C Marie Antoinette

    D Thomas Henry Hope

4. Who owned the diamond after the French royal family?

    F Jacques Celot

    G a Frenchman who was killed by wild dogs

    H Marie Antoinette

    J Thomas Henry Hope

5. What word is used to signal the last owner of the Hope diamond?

    A next

    B then

    C later

    D finally

Read On   Read "A Good Cup of Coffee." Answer the questions and look for sequence in the article.

Stated Concepts

Sometimes the main ideas of a passage are stated. Sometimes you have to figure them out. Make sure you understand the ideas that are stated when you read. Then you will understand what you read. You will also be able to figure out some ideas that are not directly stated.

Read the passage. Then circle the answer for each question.

It is hard to sneak up behind a rabbit. If you try, the rabbit will most likely rush away. It will act as if it has eyes in the back of its head. Rabbits don't have eyes in the backs of their heads. But they have the next best thing. A rabbit's eyes are on the sides of its head. With eyes like this, rabbits can see above themselves. They can see behind themselves. They can spot hunters easily. They need good eyesight because they are often hunted. Some other kinds of animals, like deer, have eyes like this.

1. What happens when someone sneaks up behind a rabbit?

   A The rabbit attacks.

   B The rabbit is surprised.

   C The rabbit stops and looks.

   D The rabbit runs away.

2. It is hard to sneak up on rabbits because

   F they have eyes in the back of their head

   G they hear well

   H they can see above and behind

   J they are often hunted

3. Rabbits' eyes are unusual because

   A they are very pale

   B they are set on the sides of the head

   C they cannot look behind the rabbit

   D they are just like those of people

4. The passage says that the eyes of rabbits and deer are helpful because

   F they hunt other animals

   G they hunt at night

   H their enemies sneak up on them

   J the animals are helpless

Read each passage. Then read each question. If the answer is stated in the passage, circle *stated*. If it is not stated, circle *not stated*.

In Juab County, Utah, there is a mountain of bugs. They are ancient bugs. You can find them easily. Put a sharp tool in a crack in the rock. Tap it with a hammer. The rock will fall open like a book. If you look, you will find a large bug. It will be two or three inches long. It is called a *trilobite*. It died 500 million years ago. You can take the sheet of rock home. If you soak it in water, you can tap out the trilobite.

1. Where can you find a trilobite?

   stated   not stated

2. How can you find a trilobite?

   stated   not stated

3. How big is a trilobite?

   stated   not stated

4. What do people learn from a trilobite?

   stated   not stated

5. What do people do with trilobites after finding them?

   stated   not stated

In Japan, the New Year is very important. People celebrate it for a whole week. The Japanese think the New Year is a time to make a fresh start. They clean their houses well. They pay old bills. They dress in their newest clothes. Children fly kites. People put pine branches on their doors. The pine wreaths send a wish. The wish is that all who see the wreathes will have a long life.

6. How long do people celebrate the New Year in Japan?

   stated   not stated

7. Why is the New Year important in Japan?

   stated   not stated

8. How did the Japanese New Year customs begin?

   stated   not stated

9. How do Japanese people show their good wishes for others at the New Year?

   stated   not stated

10. How do people in other countries celebrate the New Year?

   stated   not stated

Read the passages. Then answer the questions.

The first movies did not have sound. They did not even tell a story. They lasted only a few minutes. Still, many people went to see them. They might show a train going down a track. They might show people fighting. People were amazed to see moving pictures. The first picture with a story was made in 1903. It was called *The Life of an American Fireman*.

1. Name two ways in which the first movies differed from those of today.

   _____

2. Why did people go to see the earliest movies?

   _____

3. What was the first movie with a story about?

   _____

At one time, no one threw passes in football games. Players either ran with the ball or kicked it. In 1876 a runner got tackled. Then he threw the ball. In 1883, a player threw the ball twenty-five feet. No one really knows when passing became legal. But football fans do remember Knute Rockne. He played a great passing game. In 1912, he played for Notre Dame University. Rockne caught many passes. The team's passing confused the other teams. Soon all the teams started passing the ball.

4. How did passing in football games begin in the 1800s?

   _____

5. Who was the first football player famous for a passing game?

   _____

6. Why did many teams begin passing the ball?

   _____

D Check Up

Read the passage. Then circle the answer for each question.

During the Ice Age, many herds of horses roamed North America. They ran on the grass south of the ice. There were also horses in Asia and Europe. But after the Ice Age, no horses were left in North America. What happened to them? No one knows. Some say they all got sick and died. Others think they were eaten by other animals. These ideas do not seem right. You see, bison also lived in North America back then. But they lived through the Ice Age. They were not killed by sickness or other animals. So we don't know why the horses died. There were no more horses in the Americas until people brought them from Europe.

1. Where did horses live during the Ice Age?

   A only in Asia and Europe

   B only in North America

   C in North America, Asia, and Europe

   D nowhere

2. On what kind of land did the horses live?

   F ice

   G grass

   H desert

   J forest

3. What is one idea about why the American horses disappeared?

   A They froze to death.

   B They went to Europe.

   C They were replaced by bison.

   D They got sick.

4. The passage talks about bison because

   F they didn't disappear when horses did

   G they may have killed the horses

   H they disappeared when the horses did

   J they did not live in Europe

5. How did horses return to North America?

   A They got over their sickness.

   B They ate other animals.

   C They were brought by people from Europe.

   D No one knows.

Recalling Stated Concepts

It is important to understand and recall what you read. One way to recall what you read is to note the passage's main ideas. Ask yourself what the most important facts are. You might take notes on these. Even if you don't, recognizing the main facts will help you remember what you read.

Read the passage. Circle the answer for each question.

A beaver's tail looks like a table tennis paddle. It is flat and stiff. It has black skin and some stiff hairs. The beaver uses its tail to swim. The tail steers the animal. The tail also helps the beaver when danger is near. The animal slaps its tail on the water. The slap makes a loud noise. It warns other beavers. A beaver also uses its tail when it eats. A beaver chews on trees. Its tail props it up. So it can stand in front of a tree for a long time.

1. What does a beaver's tail look like?

   A a golf club

   B a baseball bat

   C a table tennis paddle

   D a broom

2. Which is **not** a use for the beaver's tail?

   F fighting with other animals

   G helping it stand up

   H helping it swim

   J interacting with other beavers

3. Who are the beaver's enemies?

   A other beavers

   B people

   C foxes and wolves

   D not stated

4. What does a beaver chew on?

   F grass

   G trees

   H dirt

   J not stated

5. Where do beavers live?

   A oceans

   B rain forests

   C deserts

   D not stated

Read the passage. Answer the questions with facts from the passage.

Simple hand tools are very common. They do not seem special to us. But it is important that people can use simple tools. That makes humans different from most animals. People who lived in caves first learned to make tools. They made stones into hammers or axes. That is why the time of the cave people is called the Stone Age. Stone Age people had to live where there were a lot of stones. They also had to live near animals. They hunted the animals for food. They did not know how to farm yet. Later, people used metal for tools. The tools were sharper and easier to use. Then they could farm. This was called the Iron Age.

1. What makes people different from most animals?

   _____

2. Who were the first people to make tools?

   _____

3. What did the first people make tools out of?

   _____

4. How were Stone Age people limited in where they could live?

   _____

5. What could people do after they began using metal tools?

   _____

6. What was the period with metal tools called?

   _____

C ▸ Apply

Read the passage. Then read each question. If the answer is stated in the paragraph, write the answer. If the answer is not stated, write not stated.

Rubber trees first grew in Central and South America. The people used rubber to make balls for games. In the 1800s, people from Europe found other uses for rubber. They took some trees to England. Rubber can be taken from trees when they are seven years old. It is in liquid form. It is called latex. One third of the latex is pure rubber. People make a cut in the bark of the tree. They put a cup under the cut. The liquid flows into the cup. Then the rubber is taken from the latex. A tree gives about two pounds of rubber each year. Rubber is very valuable. If we did not have rubber, we would not have tires.

1. How did people first use rubber?

   _____

   _____

2. Why was rubber used to make balls?

   _____

   _____

3. How was rubber first used in England?

   _____

   _____

4. Why is rubber valuable to people today?

   _____

   _____

5. If the natural supply ran out, what material could be substituted for rubber?

   _____

   _____

D Check Up

Read the passage. Then circle the answers to the questions.

It was almost like wearing a cage. It was a hoop skirt. Women wore them in the 1700s. They were worn in colonial America and in Europe. Skirts were long and full. Women wanted their skirts to look very full. So they wore petticoats under their skirts. A petticoat was a stiff, heavy slip. But petticoats made it hard to walk. They were heavy. So someone made a hoop skirt. It was a round piece of wire. It was worn under the skirt. The hoop worked like several petticoats, but it was much lighter.

1. When did women wear hoop skirts?

    A 1600s

    B 1700s

    C 20th century

    D not stated

2. Who invented hoop skirts?

    F a colonial American woman

    G a European woman

    H an English inventor

    J not stated

3. Which of the following is **not** identified as a petticoat problem?

    A They were stiff.

    B They were very costly.

    C They were heavy.

    D They made walking difficult.

4. Why did women wear hoop skirts?

    F to make their skirts heavier

    G to make their petticoats stiffer

    H to make their skirts look full

    J to make their waists look thinner

5. Why were hoop skirts better than petticoats?

    A They were heavier.

    B They were fuller.

    C They were lighter.

    D not stated

Read On Read "The Trail of Tears." Answer the questions and look for stated concepts in the article.

Review

Details

Details make up most of what you read. Details tell about the main idea. When you read, ask these questions:

- Which details are needed?
- Why are they needed?

He led the troops in the Mexican War. He fought again in the Black Hawk War. His nickname was "Old Rough and Ready." His real name was Zachary Taylor. He was elected president of the United States in 1849.

Details: in Mexican War, in Black Hawk War, nicknamed "Old Rough and Ready," elected president in 1849

Sequence

Sequence, or time order, is used for stories. Sequence tells the order in which events happened.

Pete folded his clothes into a suitcase. He carried his suitcase to the car. Pete's brother drove him to the airport. While he waited, he read the newspaper. After a delay, Pete boarded the plane.

Sequence: folded his clothes, took suitcase to car, drove to airport, read newspaper, boarded plane

Stated Concepts

Make sure you understand the ideas that are stated when you read.

A hot day is bad for a beehive. Heat can destroy the bees' home. But bees know how to cool off their hive. One group of bees stays outside the entrance to the hive. Another group stays inside. Both groups flap their wings quickly. This makes a cross-draft.

Stated concept: Bees cool their hive by flapping their wings and making a cross-draft.

Assessment

Read the paragraphs and circle the answer for each question.

Where do hurricanes get their names? People from a weather agency of the United Nations make up lists of names. Lists are made up for the Atlantic Ocean and the Pacific Ocean. The lists include both men's and women's names. Names are assigned alphabetically. For example, the first storm of the year gets the name that begins with A.

1. According to this passage, who makes up the list of hurricane names?

   A local weather forecasters

   B an international weather agency

   C the president of the United States

   D the people in the country affected by the storm

2. Hurricanes are named

   F in alphabetical order as they occur

   G with the same letter as the month they occur in

   H after the person who first sighted them

   J after famous people

Harvesting wheat is much easier today than it was before the 1800s. Then all the work was done by hand. Today wheat farmers use combines to harvest wheat. A combine cuts the stalks. A part of the combine rubs the grain out of the head of the wheat. Then the grain is cleaned by going through a sieve and air blasts. Finally, the grain is sent to a holding tank.

3. What happens right before the grain is sent to a holding tank?

   A The grain is cleaned.

   B The combine cuts the wheat stalks.

   C The grain is rubbed out of the head of the wheat.

   D A combine is driven through the field.

4. Why is harvesting easier today than it was before the 1800s?

   F The harvesting is done by hand.

   G The farmers work faster.

   H The wheat crops are smaller.

   J The harvesting is done by machine.

If you like the outdoors, you should know about poison ivy. You should know what it looks like so you can keep away from it. Poison ivy grows close to the ground. The leaves grow in groups of three. In summer they are green and shiny. In spring, the leaves are red. In fall, they are often orange. The plant has green flowers and whitish berries.

5. According to the paragraph, the best way to avoid poison ivy is to

    A wash your skin immediately

    B stay indoors

    C keep away from it

    D wear protective clothing

6. The berries of poison ivy are

    F red

    G orange

    H green

    J white

Where did the umbrella come from? No one knows. But we do know that the ancient Greeks and Romans were the first to use them. The word *umbrella* means "little shadow" in Latin. Women carried them to block the hot, burning sun. Hundreds of years later, people in England started using umbrellas to protect themselves from the rain.

7. Umbrellas were first used

    A as sunshades

    B as weapons

    C to keep people dry

    D to carry packages

8. Who invented the umbrella?

    F the English

    G no one knows

    H the ancient Greeks

    J the Romans

Janet Reno became the attorney general of the United States in 1993. She was appointed to the position by President Bill Clinton. Before then, Reno was the state's attorney in Dade County, Florida. She was first elected to that post in 1978. She was reelected four times.

9. Before becoming attorney general, Janet Reno was

   A a state's attorney in Florida

   B a judge in Florida

   C a college professor

   D an election official

10. How did Reno become the U.S. attorney general?

    F She was elected by the people in 1978.

    G She was appointed by the president in 1993.

    H She was reelected four times.

    J She was appointed in 1978 by other lawyers.

The Heimlich maneuver is a way to remove food blocking the windpipe. First stand behind the victim. Place your arms around the victim's waist. Make a fist and place it against the victim's abdomen, just below the ribcage. Grasp your fist with your other hand. Press upward with a quick thrust. This action forces air out of the victim's lungs. It blows the object from the windpipe.

11. What is the first thing you do when performing the Heimlich maneuver?

    A Grasp your fist with your other hand.

    B Press against the victim's abdomen with a quick thrust.

    C Stand behind the victim and place your arms around the victim's waist.

    D Make a fist and place it against the victim's abdomen.

12. To perform the Heimlich maneuver, place your fist

    F against the victim's abdomen, just below the ribcage

    G above the victim's windpipe

    H on the victim's back, just above the waist

    J just below the victim's waist

Graphic Information

Road Ramble

Study a state map. Use the map key to tell what the symbols mean. Use the scale to find out how to measure distance. Then use your map to write directions for the following trips.

1. from your town to the state capital

_____

_____

_____

2. from your town to the northern state line

_____

_____

_____

3. from your town to the nearest state park

_____

_____

_____

4. from your town to the eastern state line

_____

_____

_____

5. from your town to the closest body of water

_____

_____

_____

Time Lines

A time line is a type of diagram that shows events in the order in which they happened. On this top-to-bottom time line, the earliest event will be at the top. Fill in your daily schedule for Tuesday and Sunday. Use the lines below to write sentences comparing the two schedules. Are your schedules the same for both days? How are they alike or different?

Tuesday		**Sunday**	
7:00 A.M.		7:00 A.M.	
8:00		8:00	
9:00		9:00	
10:00		10:00	
11:00		11:00	
12:00 noon		12:00 noon	
1:00		1:00	
2:00		2:00	
3:00		3:00	
4:00		4:00	
5:00		5:00	
6:00		6:00	
7:00		7:00	
8:00		8:00	
9:00		9:00	
10:00		10:00	
11:00		11:00	
12:00 A.M.		12:00 A.M.	

Identifying Signs

When people first began to communicate, they used pictures and symbols. In math, symbols are used to tell you when to add, subtract, multiply, or divide. On signs along the roadways, symbols are used to regulate traffic or give traffic information. Symbols can also be found in public places and buildings.

Look at each sign. Match the signs with the words that tell about it.

1. _____ **A** camping

2. _____ **B** telephone

3. _____ **C** do not enter

4. _____ **D** hospital

5. _____ **E** no left turn

6. _____ **F** pedestrian crossing

7. _____ **G** bus stop

8. _____ **H** no trucks

9. _____ **I** no U-turn

10. _____ **J** railroad crossing

Look at each warning sign. What does it warn you about? Write what the sign means.

signal ahead	divided highway	bicycle route
pedestrian crossing	deer crossing	farm machinery
hill	cattle crossing	slippery when wet
	merge	

1.

_____

2.

_____

3.

_____

4.

_____

5.

_____

6.

_____

7.

_____

8.

_____

9.

_____

10.

_____

C Apply

Look at each sign. Answer the questions below.

A

D

G

J

B

E

H

C

F

I

1. Which sign tells you that roadside tables for picnics are available?

   _____

2. Which sign tells you that no trucks are allowed? _____

3. Which sign tells you to give up the right away? _____

4. Which sign tells you about a campsite where tents can be used? _____

5. Which sign tells you about a campsite where trailers can be used?

   _____

6. Which sign tells you that right turns are not allowed? _____

7. Which sign tells what highway you are on? _____

8. Which sign tells you that passing is not allowed? _____

9. Which sign tells you that there is a bump in the road? _____

10. Which sign tells you that a steep downhill grade is ahead? _____

Circle the answer that tells what the sign is.

1.
   A railroad crossing
   B telephone
   C pedestrian crossing

2.
   A hospital
   B camping
   C telephone

3.
   A no right turn
   B no U-turn
   C no trucks

4.
   A bus stop
   B airport
   C do not enter

5.
   A stop
   B look
   C slow

6.
   A pedestrian crossing
   B railroad crossing
   C bus stop

7.
   A telephone
   B camping
   C bus stop

8.
   A hospital
   B no passing zone
   C camping

9.
   A don't walk
   B wheelchair access
   C no crossing

10.
   A degrees
   B poison
   C no smoking

Reading Maps

A map is a kind of picture that shows where places are. To read a map, you need to understand its symbols.

Most maps have a map **key,** or **legend,** to tell what the symbols on the map mean.

Maps are usually drawn to scale. A **scale** shows how far apart the buildings or places on the map are.

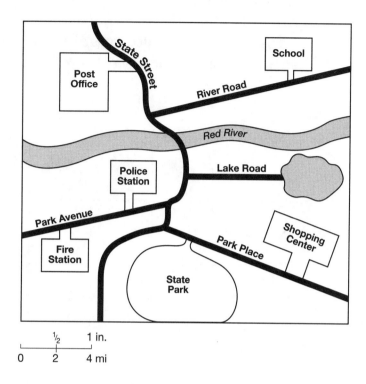

Use the information on the map to complete the sentences.

1. The school is on _____.

2. It is _____ miles from State Street.

3. The police station is on _____.

4. The park entrance is _____ miles from State Street.

5. The shopping center is on _____.

6. It is _____ miles from State Street.

7. The post office is on _____.

8. The fire station is on _____.

Look at the map key. It tells what the symbols on the map mean. The letters on the side of the map and the numbers across the top are called **coordinates.** Coordinates give the location of a specific place. Look for the Dolphin Show in A2.

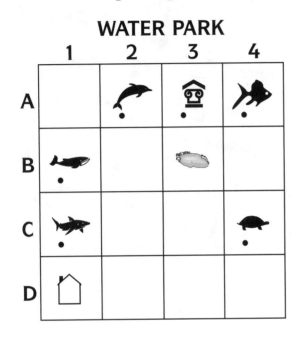

WATER PARK

Key

Information

Lake

Turtle Island

Dolphin Show

Fish Food Shop

Sea Hunt Museum

Whale Walk

Shark Alley

yards   100   200

inches   1   2

Use the map to answer the questions.

1. What does the symbol ⌂ stand for? _____

2. What does the symbol 🐟 stand for? _____

3. What does the symbol 🐬 stand for? _____

4. How far is 🐬 from the Turtle Island? _____

5. How far is it from the Fish Food Shop to Whale Walk? _____

6. How far is it from the Sea Hunt Museum to Shark Alley? _____

7. Write the coordinates for the lake. _____

8. Write the coordinates for Sea Hunt Museum. _____

9. What is located at coordinates C1? _____

10. What is located at coordinates C4? _____

C ▸ Apply

Look at the map. Write the answer to each question.

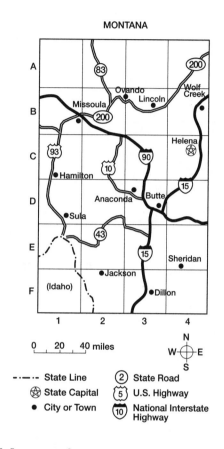

MONTANA

1. What is the capital of Montana? _____

2. What kind of road is 83? _____

3. What kind of road is 15? _____

4. About how far is Sula from the Idaho border? _____

5. About how far is it by road from Butte to Wolf Creek? _____

6. How many cities are shown on this map of Montana? _____

7. What are the coordinates for Sheridan? _____

8. What roads would you take from Lincoln to Butte? _____

9. What three roads are in coordinate B2? _____

10. Write the city located at these coordinates.

   C1 _____   B1 _____

   C4 _____   E4 _____

Ridgeville

	1	2	3	4	5
A	Book store •	Library •	Restaurant •		Theater •
B	State house •	Monument •			Statue •
C	Parking lot •			City park •	
D	Doctor's office •	Office building •	Grocery store •	Clothing store •	Apartment house •

feet 0 25 50 75 100

|--|--|--|--|

inches 0 $\frac{1}{2}$ 1

Complete the index. Write the letter and the number of the coordinates for each location.

1. Apartment house _____

2. Book store _____

3. City park _____

4. Clothing store _____

5. Doctor's office _____

6. Grocery store _____

7. Library _____

8. Monument _____

9. Office building _____

10. Parking lot _____

Measure each distance from dot to dot. Choose the correct measurement.

11. From the statue to the monument

    A 25 feet

    B 175 feet

    C 350 feet

12. From the state house to city park

    A 2 feet

    B 100 feet

    C 200 feet

Read On   Read "Ellis Island." Answer the questions and draw maps and signs related to the article.

A ► Introduce

Using Graphs

Graphs are a way to show information in a picture that makes it easier to understand. There are several types of graphs.

Line graphs give a picture for comparing numbers. A grid is used to make a line graph. The numbers on the left side show the frequency. In this case, it is the number of people who use cell phones.

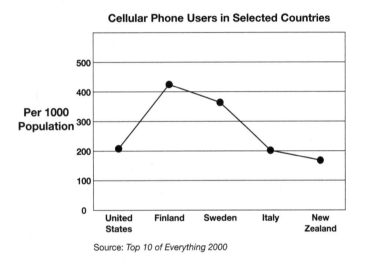

Cellular Phone Users in Selected Countries

Source: *Top 10 of Everything 2000*

1. Which country has the most cell phone users per one thousand population?

_____

2. Which country has the fewest cell phone users per one thousand population?

_____

3. Which country has 2 times as many cell phone users as the United States?

_____

4. Which country has just over 350 users per 1000?

_____

5. Which country has almost the same number of users per one thousand people as the United States?

_____

B▶ Practice

Bar graphs give an easy way to compare increases and decreases over time. These two bar graphs show that the number of people not counted by the Unites States census have been decreasing.

In this first bar graph, the numbers on the left side show the number of people in millions. The numbers along the bottom show the years used. This is a **vertical bar graph** since the bars go up and down.

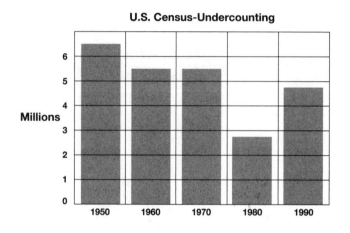

In a **horizontal bar graph** the bars go across the graph. In this bar graph, the numbers along the left side show the years. The numbers at the bottom show the number of people in millions.

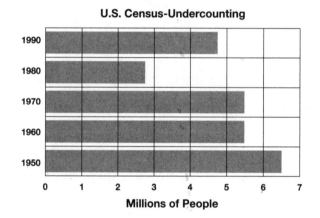

Study the bar graphs and answer the questions.

1. In which year were the most people not counted? _____

2. In which two years were about the same number of people not counted?

   _____

3. How many people were missed in 1950? _____

4. How many people were missed in 1990? _____

5. In which year were the fewest number of people not counted?

   _____

C ▶ Apply

Circle graphs show parts in relation to the whole. The parts look like slices of pie. Since a circle graph looks like a pie cut into pieces, it is often called a *pie chart*.

The whole graph equals 100 percent. Each of the pieces shows the percent for that part. When all the percents are added together, the total is 100 percent.

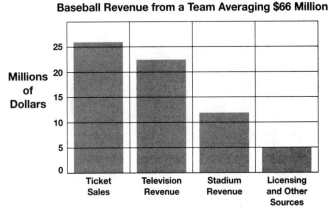

Graph A

Baseball Revenue Sources

Graph B

Baseball Revenue from a Team Averaging $66 Million

Source: information from World Book

Circle graphs and bar graphs give different kinds of information. Study the graphs and answer the questions.

1. How much money is earned from ticket sales? _____

   Which graph did you use? _____

2. What percentage does television revenue supply? _____

   Which graph did you use? _____

3. How much money is earned from television revenue? _____

   Which graph did you use? _____

4. Which source gives the smallest amount of revenue? _____

   Which graph did you use? _____

5. Which source gives the largest amount of revenue? _____

   Which graph did you use? _____

D # Check Up

Circle the answer to each question.

Graph A

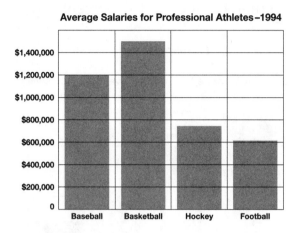

Average Salaries for Professional Athletes–1994

Source: information from World Book

Graph B

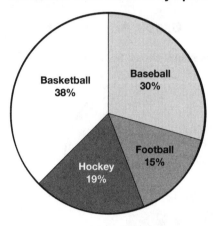

Percent of Total Salaries by Sport

1. Which sport has an average salary of one million two hundred thousand dollars?

   A baseball

   B basketball

   C hockey

   D football

2. Which sport has an average salary of seven hundred fifty thousand dollars?

   F baseball

   G basketball

   H hockey

   J football

3. Which sport pays the second highest average salaries?

   A baseball

   B basketball

   C hockey

   D football

4. Which sport pays the highest average salary?

   F baseball

   G basketball

   H hockey

   J football

5. Which sport pays the lowest average salary?

   A baseball

   B basketball

   C hockey

   D football

6. Which sport represents 19% of the total salaries?

   F baseball

   G basketball

   H hockey

   J football

Using Graphs

Use the graphs to answer the questions.

Graph A

Favorite Sports of Students at Home School

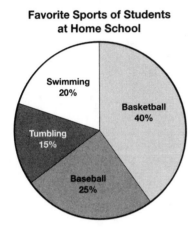

Graph B

After-School Sports at Home School

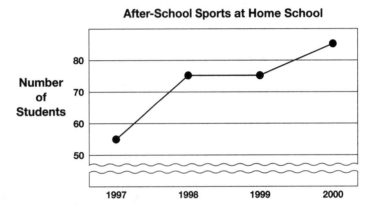

Runners at Home School

Graph C

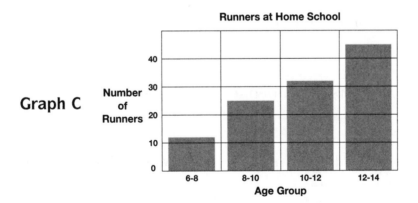

1. What kind of graph is Graph A? _____

2. What kind of graph is Graph B? _____

3. What kind of graph is Graph C? _____

4. Which graph shows how many children play after-school sports at Home School? _____

5. What is the favorite sport of students at Home School? _____

6. Which age group has the fewest runners? _____

Use the line graph to answer the questions.

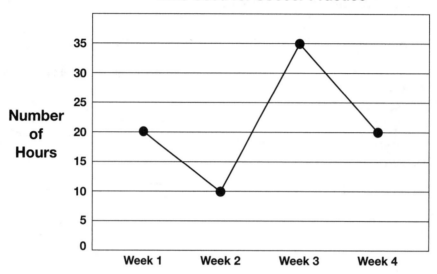

Time Used for Soccer Practice

1. During which week did the team practice the most?

   _____

2. What was the least numbers of hours practiced in one week?

   _____

3. How many fewer hours did the team practice in Week 2 than in Week 3?

   _____

4. What is the difference between the greatest and the least number of hours practiced?

   _____

5. During which weeks did the team practice the same number of hours?

   _____

6. Which week did the number of hours of practice drop by 15 from the week before?

   _____

◆C Apply

Use the graphs to answer the questions.

Graph A

How Hill Valley People Get to Work

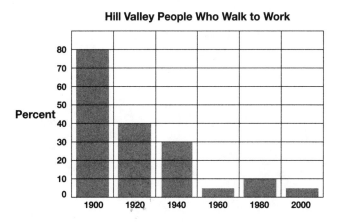

Graph B

Hill Valley People Who Walk to Work

1. What percent of Hill Valley people go to work by train? _____

2. What is a true statement about Hill Valley people? Circle your answer.

   A There are fewer train riders than bus riders.

   B Train riders make up more than one-half of the workers.

   C There are as many train riders as there are bus riders and car riders together.

3. Which graph shows the change in the percent of people who walk to work?
   _____

4. What is a true statement about Hill Valley people? Circle your answer.

   A The percentage of walkers has always gone up.

   B The percentage of walkers has gone down since 1900.

   C The percentage of walkers has stayed the same from 1900 to 2000.

5. What kind of graph would you create to show the change in bus riders from 1900 to 2000? _____

◆D Check Up

Use the graphs to answer the questions.

Graph A

Favorite Composers of Audiences

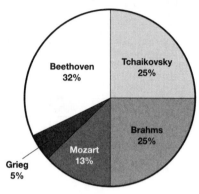

Graph B

Average Size of Audiences for Royal Orchestra Tour

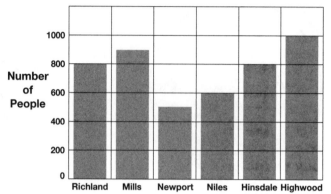

1. Which towns had the same average size audiences?

   A Niles, Hinsdale

   B Newport, Niles

   C Richland, Hinsdale

2. Which was the average size of audiences for Newport?

   A 800

   B 500

   C 600

3. Which composer was the least favorite of the audiences?

   A Grieg

   B Mozart

   C Brahms

4. Which composer was the favorite of audiences?

   A Brahms

   B Beethoven

   C Tchaikovsky

5. What percent of the audiences liked Tchaikovsky?

   A 25%

   B 35%

   C 15%

6. Which was the average size of audiences for Highwood?

   A 800

   B 1000

   C 900

Read On   Read "Building a Budget." Answer the questions and use information in the article to create graphs.

 **Introduce**

Consumer Materials

If you are looking for a job, you may look in newspaper **want ads.** There you will find listings for many different types of jobs. The listings are usually in alphabetical order according to the kind of job. Often abbreviations, or shortened forms of words, are used in the ads. You need to know what these abbreviations stand for in order to understand the ads.

> **CASHIERS** needed ASAP for conv. stores in various locations
> P/T—hrs: 7–10 wk nights, 7–11 Sat. and Sun. $6.20 per hr
> No exp. nec. Must be responsible with gd. attde.
> Apply: Jim Hanley, P.O.B. 3121, Bloomington, MN 55420   EOE

Look at the ad shown. Then match the abbreviations to the words they stand for.

_____ 1. ASAP	**A** experience necessary
_____ 2. conv.	**B** week
_____ 3. P/T	**C** Minnesota
_____ 4. hr	**D** convenience
_____ 5. wk	**E** Saturday
_____ 6. Sat.	**F** good attitude
_____ 7. Sun.	**G** as soon as possible
_____ 8. exp. nec.	**H** Post Office Box
_____ 9. gd. attde.	**I** Sunday
_____ 10. P.O.B.	**J** part-time
_____ 11. MN	**K** equal opportunity employer
_____ 12. EOE	**L** hour

B Practice

You see an ad in the paper. You decide to apply for the job. What do you do? It often depends on the ad. Some ads suggest that you call, apply in person, or fax or write. If you fax or write, the employer sees you first through your writing. You need to be able to write a letter in which you tell something about yourself and why you are the person for the job. Everything—from spelling to grammar to information—in your letter needs to be correct. Look at the sample and write a letter of your own to Mr. Hanley in answer to the ad on page 105.

Mitchell Grandy
2241 South Waverly Avenue
Bloomington, MN 55420
1-612-555-7198

Sender's Address: Begin the letter with your name, address, and telephone number.

September 14, 2001

Date: Write the date.

Mr. Jim Hanley
P.O.B. 3121
Bloomington, MN 55420

Inside Address: Provide the complete address of the person or company that published the ad.

Dear Mr. Hanley:

Greeting: Greet the person.

Your advertisement for cashiers in the *Minneapolis Star-Tribune* caught my attention. I am interested in one of the positions you have open.

Body of Letter: Name the job and where you saw the ad for it.

For the past two summers, I have been an employee at Aver's Pet Shop. My responsibilities included caring for the animals, helping customers, and making sales. Now I am looking for an evening position so that I can attend classes during the day.

Give some information about yourself.

I am a conscientious employee with good math skills. I enjoy working with people. I can provide references from Ms. Aver at the pet shop.

Please send me an application or call me at 555-7198 to arrange an interview. I look forward to hearing from you soon. Thank you for considering my application.

Ask for an application or an interview.

Sincerely,

Closing: Close your letter.

Mitchell Grandy

Mitchell Grandy

Signature: Sign and type your name.

◆C Apply

Look at the following advertisement. Answer the questions and write a letter.

HELP WANTED

Office Assistant for small insurance agency. Responsibilities include greeting customers, answering phones, and preparing estimates. Must type 60 words per min. F/T 9–5 Mon.–Fri. No weekends. Complete med. and dental plan. $8.50 per hr. Ms. Sorrell, Campden Agency, 891 Tover Ave., Kearny, NJ 07032   EOE

1. What position is being advertised? _____

2. What company is looking for help? _____

3. To whom would you address your letter of application? _____

4. What skills are needed to do the job? _____

5. How much does the job pay? _____

6. What employee benefits are listed? _____

7. What does the office assistant do? _____

8. What are the working hours? _____

9. When is the office open? _____

10. Imagine you are answering this or another Help Wanted ad. Write a letter on a separate sheet of paper. Tell why you are interested in the position. Tell why you would make a good employee.

◆D Check Up

Circle the answer for each question.

1. What does P/T stand for?

   A presently

   B parent

   C part-time

   D person's title

2. What is the abbreviation for equal opportunity employer?

   F Equop

   G EOE

   H EOA

   J OpEm

3. Which of the following is an employee benefit?

   A medical plan

   B pay

   C work hours

   D responsibilities

4. How do you end a letter answering a want ad?

   F with the date

   G by signing it

   H with the business's address

   J with a greeting

5. What would be a good closing for a letter answering a want ad?

   A Your friend,

   B Gratefully yours,

   C Love,

   D Sincerely,

6. Which of the following is an abbreviation for a day of the week?

   F hr

   G wk

   H Sun.

   J MN

7. Where is the name and address of the person receiving the letter found?

   A date

   B sender's address

   C body of the letter

   D inside address

8. What does F/T mean in want ads?

   F full-time

   G free time

   H fair trade

   J first take

9. How are the jobs in want ads usually listed?

   A by number

   B by location

   C alphabetically

   D by amount of salary

10. What is the abbreviation for Post Office Box?

    F P.Of.

    G B.P.O.

    H O.P.B.

    J P.O.B.

A ▸ Introduce

Consumer Materials

You have a job interview. You want to make a good impression. Your appearance and behavior are the first things the interviewer will note. Think about what you should and should not do during an interview.

Read the list. Write *yes* next to actions that you should do before and during an interview. Write *no* next to actions you should not do.

_____ 1. Greet the receptionist politely.

_____ 2. Lean on the interviewer's desk.

_____ 3. Look at the interviewer throughout the interview.

_____ 4. Check your watch throughout the interview.

_____ 5. Bring a list of references, people the interviewer can talk to about you.

_____ 6. Bring a magazine from the reception area into the interview room.

_____ 7. Address the interviewer by his or her last name.

_____ 8. Look at papers on the interviewer's desk.

_____ 9. Arrive late for the interview.

_____ 10. Chew gum.

_____ 11. Shake the interviewer's hand when you are introduced.

_____ 12. Ask about job responsibilities.

_____ 13. Talk about your plans for the evening.

_____ 14. Tell about your skills and abilities.

_____ 15. Ask for a cup of coffee.

_____ 16. Answer your cell phone during the interview.

_____ 17. Bring copies of your resumé to the interview.

_____ 18. Remain standing until the interviewer invites you to sit down.

◆B Practice

Many interviewers ask the same type of questions. You should think about these questions and be prepared to answer them.

Think of the type of job you are qualified for. Name the job. Then read the following questions. Think about what you could say in response to the question. Write some ideas.

1. What skills and strengths do you have that will help you do the job?

   _____

   _____

   _____

2. Why do you want to work here?

   _____

   _____

   _____

3. What do you know or want to know about this company?

   _____

   _____

   _____

4. What do you see yourself doing five or more years from now?

   _____

   _____

   _____

5. Why did you leave your last job?

   _____

   _____

   _____

 **Apply**

Most employers have application forms. You will be asked to complete the form before you are interviewed. Answer all questions on the form.

Complete this sample application form.

APPLICATION FOR EMPLOYMENT

Date _____

Personal Information

Name _____
      Last   First   Middle Initial

Address _____
         Street

_____
         City   State   ZIP

Telephone Number _____

Social Security Number _____

Citizen of the United States: Yes   No

Are you related to anyone working for this company?   Yes   No
If so, please name the employee and his or her department.

_____

Employment Desired

Position _____

Date that you can begin working _____

Have you ever applied for employment with this company before?   Yes   No

If so, where and when did you apply? _____

Education

Name and Location of School	No. of Years Attended	Graduation Date
College	_____	_____
Trade or Business School	_____	_____
High School or GED	_____	_____

D Check Up

Circle the answer for each question.

1. Which of the following is something you should do during an interview?

   A chew gum

   B lean on the interviewer's desk

   C shake the interviewer's hand

   D answer your cell phone

2. Which of the following is **not** information asked for on a job application form?

   F Social Security Number

   G number of brothers and sisters

   H home address

   J name and location of schools attended

3. Which of the following is a question that an interviewer probably would **not** ask you?

   A Why did you leave your last job?

   B Do you attend worship services every week?

   C What do you see yourself doing five or more years from now?

   D What skills and abilities do you have?

4. Which of the following is something you should **not** do during an interview?

   F tell about your skills and abilities

   G ask about job responsibilities

   H check your watch constantly

   J look at the interviewer throughout the interview

5. Which of the following is information you would expect a job application form to ask?

   A your weight

   B the number of children you have

   C your favorite foods

   D the position you are applying for

Read On Read "Armchair Shopping." Answer the comprehension and mail-order questions at the end of the article.

Signs

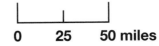

Symbols on signs give information.

You see this sign at an airport. What does it mean?

_____

Maps

A map is a kind of picture that
shows where places are.

0   25   50 miles

Use the map key or legend to tell what the symbols on a map mean. Use
this scale to determine distance. If the road from Glenview to Millville is
2 inches long, how many miles is that?

_____

Graphs

Reading a graph helps you compare
things easily.

Three types of graphs are line, bar,
and circle graphs.

What percentage of people rate New York
as their favorite vacation place?

_____

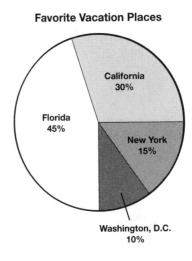

Favorite Vacation Places

California 30%

Florida 45%

New York 15%

Washington, D.C. 10%

Consumer Materials

When you read newspaper want ads, you need to understand what the
abbreviations stand for.

What are the working hours? _____

What benefits does the job offer? _____

P/T Office Help needed ASAP
Hrs: 10–2 M, W, F
Comp. exp. nec., $9.25 per hr
Med. benefits; pd. vacation, increase after 90 days.
Hampton Insurance Agency
145 Main Street
Vineland, IL 06038   EOE

Circle the answer that tells what the symbol means.

1.
   A telephone
   B hospital
   C school crossing zone
   D bus stop

2.
   F wheelchair access
   G school
   H airport
   J camping

3.
   A stop
   B yield
   C merge
   D do not enter

4.
   F no bicycles
   G no dogs
   H no smoking
   J no eating

5.
   A pedestrian crossing
   B deer crossing
   C railroad crossing
   D fire lane

6.
   F no right turn
   G don't walk
   H no U-turn
   J no left turn

7.
   A no parking
   B hospital
   C handicapped parking
   D do not enter

8.
   F dogs must be on a leash
   G no dogs
   H no skateboarding
   J recycle materials

9.
   A no smoking
   B one-way
   C yield
   D recycle materials

10.
   F no passing zone
   G don't walk
   H walk
   J wheelchair access

Use the map and circle the answer.

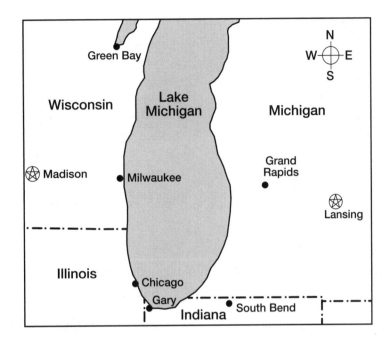

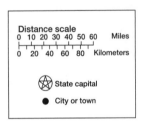

11. What city is almost directly west of Grand Rapids, Michigan?

    A Chicago, Illinois

    B Gary, Indiana

    C Lansing, Michigan

    D Milwaukee, Wisconsin

12. The distance between Gary, Indiana, and South Bend, Indiana, is about

    F 160 miles

    G 60 miles

    H 120 miles

    J 100 miles

13. The capital of Wisconsin is

    A Madison

    B Chicago

    C Green Bay

    D Milwaukee

14. Which city is located about 30 miles from Chicago, Illinois?

    F Green Bay, Wisconsin

    G Grand Rapids, Michigan

    H Gary, Indiana

    J Lansing, Michigan

Use the graphs and circle the answer.

Graph 1

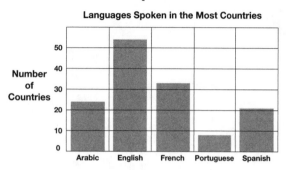

Languages Spoken in the Most Countries

Source: *Top 10 of Everything 2000*

Graph 2

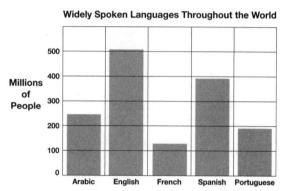

Widely Spoken Languages Throughout the World

Source: *Top 10 of Everything 2000*

15. Graph 1 is a

   A circle graph

   B time line

   C bar graph

   D line graph

16. Which language is spoken in the fewest countries?

   F English

   G Portuguese

   H Arabic

   J Spanish

17. How many people speak Arabic?

   A about 250,000,000

   B about 200,000,000

   C about 500,000,000

   D about 400,000,000

Graph 3

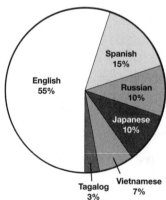

Languages Spoken in Mill Valley

18. Which language is spoken by the fewest number of people in Mill Valley?

   F Russian

   G Spanish

   H Tagalog

   J Vietnamese

Constructing Meaning

Character Traits

What traits do you look for in people? Do you look for the same qualities in a friend as you do in an employee or teacher? Read the following words and think of what they mean. Then write each word below the person it might apply to.

calm	loyal	knowledgeable
honest	on time	agreeable
patient	organized	responsible
fun	fair	kind

friend   **employee**   **teacher**

_____   _____   _____

_____   _____   _____

_____   _____   _____

_____   _____   _____

Choose one of the lists. Use each of the words in a sentence that tells how the person puts that character trait into action.

_____

_____

_____

_____

Action—Reaction

Do you ever ask yourself why something happens? The reason something happens is the cause. But sometimes a cause can have different effects. Do you look at things positively or negatively? Think about how you would react to each of the following situations and fill out the chart.

Positive Effect	Cause	Negative Effect
	Your best friend moves way.	
	You get the promotion at work that you wanted.	
	You can't afford concert tickets.	
	The store no longer carries the CD player you have been saving for.	
	You miss your bus.	

Recognizing Character Traits

When you read a fiction story, you will meet characters. You may also read articles about real people. It helps to think about what each person is like. You can pick out a person's character traits in a few different ways:

- what a person says
- what a person does
- what other people say about the person

Read each sentence about a person. Then write one or more character traits for the person from the list.

adventurous	wise	supportive	brave	peace-loving	inventive
creative	helpful	intelligent	bold	artistic	

1. Clara Barton brought the Red Cross to the United States.

_____

2. George Washington led a small, poor American army against the British.

_____

3. Martha Graham invented modern dance.

_____

4. Thomas A. Edison made the first practical electric light bulb.

_____

5. Ernest Hemingway enjoyed hunting animals in Africa.

_____

Read the passage. Then answer the questions.

William Sidis was born in 1898. He was very bright. His father wanted to show how fast a child could learn. So he made William study math, French, and other subjects. At age nine, the boy was ready for college. Harvard would not let him in until he was eleven. At college, William was a whiz. But soon William broke down. He took a long rest away from school. When he went back, he was not happy. As an adult, William wanted to be left alone. He did not talk to his parents. He had many unusual interests. He died at the age of forty-six. He had no friends.

1. Which word best describes William's father?

   A kind

   B pushy

   C relaxed

   D violent

2. As a child, William was

   F playful

   G athletic

   H witty

   J studious

3. William's unhappiness seemed to be caused by

   A his intelligence

   B his laziness

   C the college he attended

   D being pushed to succeed

4. Which word best describes William as an adult?

   F wise

   G odd

   H successful

   J bored

C Apply

Read the passage. Then answer the questions with character traits from the list.

selfish	patient	talented	clever	resourceful
lively	brave	shy	creative	lazy
charming	independent	original	angry	

As a young boy, Hans Christian Andersen spent most of his time pretending. He had few friends. He liked to play alone with his toy theater. When he was seven, his parents took him to see a play. From then on, he wanted to be an actor. At age fourteen, Hans set out on his own. For three years, he tried to get jobs acting. He was told many times that he had no talent for it. He went back to school. He was a good student, but he was lonely. He wrote about his feelings. When he was thirty, Andersen started writing fairy tales. He sold them to make money. Today his tales are read by people all over the world.

1. Write two words that describe Hans as a child.

   _____

2. Write a word that describes Hans at the age of fourteen.

   _____

3. Write a word that describes Hans when he was trying to be an actor.

   _____

4. Write a word that describes Hans at the age of thirty.

   _____

5. Hans had few friends. What character trait do you think caused this?

   _____

Read the passage. Circle the answer for each question.

Wheat and corn flakes were first made by Dr. John Kellogg. He worked with his brother, Will. They ran a center in Michigan to care for the sick. They wanted their patients to have fresh vegetables. They liked natural foods. They tried different ways to cook grains. One day, they put some boiled wheat in the oven. They were called away from the kitchen. When they returned, they thought the wheat had cooked too long. They decided to run it through rollers. They found that thin flakes formed. They had discovered how to make corn, rice, and wheat flakes. Will Kellogg formed a company to market the flakes. By the early 1900s, W. K. Kellogg was a household name.

1. The Kelloggs' attitudes toward their patients shows they were

   A greedy

   B kind

   C trusting

   D selfish

2. The Kelloggs' search for better foods shows they were

   F curious

   G clumsy

   H foolish

   J lazy

3. The Kelloggs' experience with the boiled wheat shows they were

   A impatient

   B inventive

   C helpless

   D careless

4. Judging from this passage, a good way to succeed in **business** is to

   F focus on making money

   G try to make better products

   H not care about other people

   J not care about new things

5. John and Will Kellogg **are best** known as

   A doctors

   B inventors

   C inventors and businessmen

   D health care experts

Recognizing Character Traits

Read the following passage.

Louis Armstrong, the "King of Jazz," started playing music when he was a child in New Orleans. He and three friends formed a group. They had to practice their songs in alleys and vacant lots. They sang on street corners. People tossed them coins. Later, Armstrong met a man, Peter Davis. Davis taught the boy to play drums, horn, bugle, and cornet. It is hard to get a job as a musician. But finally Louis got a job in a band. His horn playing and singing made him famous. He made many hit records. Now the whole world knows Armstrong's jazz.

What does the passage say about Armstrong's character? First of all, playing music as a child shows that Armstrong was very **talented**. Practicing in alleys and vacant lots shows that he was **hard-working** and **determined**. Practicing for years before getting a musical job shows that he was **patient.**

Read each sentence. Write a character trait shown by the person in the sentence.

1. Eleanor Roosevelt helped her husband campaign for president after he was struck by polio.

   _____

2. Martin Luther King, Jr., told African Americans not to use violence.

   _____

3. Former President Jimmy Carter has helped build houses for needy people.

   _____

B Practice

Read the passage. Then circle the answers to the questions.

A. A. Milne wrote stories and poems for children. His son, Christopher Robin, was the subject of some of his books. Milne watched his son play. Then he wrote stories about the boy's play adventures. He wrote about the stuffed bear, Winnie-the-Pooh. The books were very popular. When he was little, Christopher got attention because of his father's books. He liked the attention. But his feelings changed. Other boys teased him at school. He began to hate his fame. But around that time, his father stopped writing about him. Today, Christopher Robin Milne runs a bookstore. The books his father wrote are classics for children.

1. Which word is **not** a good one to describe A. A. Milne?

   A imaginative

   B fanciful

   C strict

   D creative

2. How did Milne feel about his son Christopher?

   F He was spoiled.

   G He was a genius.

   H He was boring.

   J He was interesting.

3. Why did Christopher's feelings about his father's books change?

   A He didn't like his father anymore.

   B He was embarrassed about being in children's books.

   C He didn't like his father's writing.

   D The books were not popular anymore.

4. Christopher began to hate his fame when he was ten. What can you conclude about Christopher?

   F He did not like his father's work.

   G He got upset too easily.

   H He was a normal ten year old.

   J He was too serious.

5. How did Christopher's childhood affect his adult life?

   A He hated books.

   B He disliked his father.

   C He didn't want to grow up.

   D He worked with books.

C ▸ Apply

Read the passage. Then answer the questions with character traits from the list.

selfish	patient	talented	clever	resourceful
lively	brave	shy	creative	lazy
charming	independent	original	angry	

Belle Boyd was a Confederate spy in the Civil War. She became a spy after she shot a Union soldier in her home in Virginia. At seventeen she learned all about secret codes. She used her skills. She stole secrets from the northern armies. Northern troops caught Belle three times. They let her go each time. The third time, a young Union officer named Sam Hardinge was her guard. He fell in love with her. They ran away to England and got married. But Hardinge soon died. Belle went back to the U. S. She became an actress. She became famous for her speeches about her life as a spy.

1. Shooting a Union soldier in her home shows that Belle was _____.

2. Belle became an expert in secret codes. Write a word that describes this part of Belle's character. _____

3. Belle's guard fell in love with her. Belle must have been very _____.

4. Belle became an actress and a speaker. This shows that she was _____.

5. Belle had several different careers. She was _____.

◆D Check Up

Read the passage. Circle the answers to the questions.

Muhammad Ali was the heavyweight boxing champ. He was a great athlete. He had the hand and foot speed to play almost any sport. He chose to box. As a young man, he won an Olympic gold medal. He was the heavyweight champ three times. Ali became known all over the world. He spouted funny poems, mostly about himself. Ali had a serious side. He refused to go to war in the late 1960s because of his religious beliefs. He lost the title for that act. But he gained the respect of many people.

1. Muhammad Ali's poems show that he

   A was a great writer

   B had a good sense of humor

   C was very intelligent

   D was a great athlete

2. Ali would not go to war. This shows that he was

   F lazy

   G determined

   H brave

   J selfish

3. In general, Muhammad Ali's personality was

   A likable

   B violent

   C unhappy

   D serious

4. Muhammad Ali is best known for

   F his poetry

   G winning a boxing title

   H winning an Olympic gold medal

   J his religious beliefs

5. Ali's story shows that

   A boxing is the best sport for an athlete

   B athletes don't have to fight in wars

   C athletes with strong characters earn the most respect

   D Olympic athletes usually become pro athletes

Read On   Read "The Fabulous Miss Bly." Answer the questions and look for character traits in the article.

Identifying Main Idea

When you read a story or article, you read many details. To understand what you read, find the main idea that links all the details.

A group of lions is called a pride. A pride is made up of one to three males, several females, and cubs. Some of the pride members hunt for food in one spot, some in another. A pride hunts in an area of 15 to 150 square miles. Strangers that enter the pride's grounds are chased out or killed.

This passage tells some details about how lions live. It tells the name for a group of lions. It tells how many animals are in a pride. What is the main idea that links all these details? It could be stated "Lions live and work together in a community." When you find the main idea of a passage, you find the idea that connects all the details.

Read the passage. Then circle the letter of the sentence that tells the passage's main idea.

Do you know why food is sometimes kept in cans? Cans keep food fresh. If food is spoiled, it is not safe to eat. Food spoils when germs get to it. There are germs in the air. They can land on the food and grow on it. These germs can harm people. When food is put into cans, most of the air is sealed out. That is why the food stays fresh.

A Germs are carried in the air.

B Germs make people sick.

C Cans protect food from germs.

D Cans make food taste better.

B Practice

Read each passage. If the underlined sentence is the main idea of the passage, write *main idea* on the line. If it is a detail, write *detail*.

1. Riddles are puzzling questions. Today, they are told for fun. For instance, when is a door not a door? (when it is ajar) What flies forever and rests never? (the wind) But long ago, riddles were very important to people. Ancient priests answered questions with riddles. They used riddles to give advice to kings. Riddle contests were held at Greek and Roman parties. Sometimes a person would die if he or she did not give the right answer.

   _____

2. Fiddler crabs are colorful shellfish. Their name comes from the male crab. It has one very large claw. He holds it as if it were a violin. Female fiddlers have two small claws. But the male has one small one and one large one.

   _____

3. Crows are clever birds. They can get food away from a dog. A team of three crows dives toward a dog that has food. Two crows fly about to confuse the dog. The third crow dashes in and takes the food.

   _____

4. In August 1926, New York City held a big parade. It was for a nineteen-year-old American, Gertrude Ederle. Ederle was the first woman to swim across the English Channel. She also beat the record by two hours. She swam across in fourteen hours and thirty-one minutes. It was a twenty-two mile swim. The waves were rough. The water was cold. Darkness fell before she finished her swim.

   _____

C ▶ Apply

In your own words, state the main idea of each passage.

1. Birds rarely fight over food. Sparrows eat seeds. Geese love grass. Woodpeckers find bugs in tree trunks. Other birds hunt for them among the leaves. Still others pull them from the ground.

   _____

   _____

2. The great hunter of the early dinosaurs was allosaurus. Other dinosaurs were scared of this giant. Allosaurus was a meat-eater. It had huge jaws and teeth like knives. Allosaurus walked on its back legs. It could leap and strike very quickly. With its sharp claws it tore its prey to bits.

   _____

   _____

3. Today's doughnuts are round cakes with holes in the center. They are fried in fat. The cakes were first made in Holland. They were called "nuts" because of their shape. Dutch settlers brought the cakes to America. An American invented the doughnut hole. He cut a hole in the cakes to make them lighter.

   _____

   _____

4. Buildings keep getting taller. It is good that most tall buildings have elevators. Elevators are very simple. They are big boxes. The boxes hang by a steel cable. The cable winds around a pulley. A person pushes a switch in the elevator. That turns on a motor. The motor makes the pulley run. The pulley winds the cable. The elevator moves.

   _____

   _____

Read each passage. Circle the answer for each question.

The first boats were made of tree trunks. A person could sit on the trunk and float. After a time, someone made a raft. He tied many trunks together. Later, people scooped out the trunks of trees. This made safer boats. The American Indians called these canoes.

1. Which sentence tells the main idea of this passage?

   A Tree trunks are the best material for boats.

   B Indians found many uses for canoes.

   C People have used tree trunks as boats for many years.

   D Boats with scooped out trunks are safest.

Sleep rests our bodies. During sleep, our heartbeat slows down. Our muscles loosen and relax. But scientists have found other reasons for sleep. They say sleep is needed for the brain and nervous system.

2. What is the main idea of the passage?

   F Scientists have studied sleep.

   G Our nervous system needs sleep.

   H Our bodies change when we sleep.

   J Our bodies need sleep for many reasons.

In A.D. 79, the city of Pompeii, Italy, was a resort. Rich Romans went there to relax. The city had been built near a dead volcano, Mount Vesuvius. But one day the volcano erupted. It threw hot ash and stone on the city. It filled the air with poison. Pompeii was destroyed.

3. This passage is mainly about

   A rich Romans

   B volcanoes

   C the city of Pompeii

   D ancient Roman life

The mouse deer was well named. It has a body like a deer. It has a head like a mouse. It is about the size of a rabbit. But mouse deer are neither mice nor deer. They are shy animals. They only come out at night.

4. What is the main idea of the passage?

   F Mouse deer are very shy.

   G The name of the mouse deer describes the animal.

   H A mouse deer has the body of a deer.

   J Mouse deer and rabbits are the same size.

Finding the Main Idea

When you read, look for the main idea. Sometimes the main idea of a paragraph is stated in the very first sentence. Or it may be stated in another part of the paragraph. Sometimes the main idea is not stated directly. Try to figure out the main idea of a passage. Then check to see if all the details support the main idea. Do all the details fit? If not, try stating the main idea in a different way.

Read each passage. Then circle the letter that states the main idea.

1. No one knows for sure when the wheel came about. Some say it was first used as a potter's wheel. Others think it was used as the wheel of a cart. The wheel led to many changes. Farming got easier. People did not have to walk everywhere. The wheel led to a machine called a pulley. With a pulley, people could lift big stones. They could make buildings with the stones.

   A Thanks to wheels, people could ride on carts.

   B Wheels helped people farm better.

   C The wheel helped people in many ways.

   D No one knows when people first used wheels.

2. Linen is a light, woven cloth. It is made from the stems of the flax plant. The dried stalks of the plant are soaked in water. Then the fibers are taken from the stems. They are dried again. The finest fibers are used for weaving. Linen is used for summer clothing and tablecloths. Ireland is known for its fine linen.

   F Linen should be worn in summer.

   G Fibers are taken from flax stems.

   H You can buy good linen in Ireland.

   J Linen is a cloth made from flax.

Read each passage. If the underlined sentence is the main idea of the passage, write *main idea* on the line. If it is a detail, write *detail*.

1. In some places, there is hot water deep under the ground. When the water bubbles up, it is called a hot spring. When it shoots into the air, it is called a geyser. In Iceland, there is a lot of hot water under the ground. In the capital city, hot water is piped from the ground. It is used in homes and schools.

   _____

2. One of the first space travelers was a dog. Her name was Laika. In 1957, Laika took off in a Russian rocket. The rocket was called *Sputnik II*. Laika flew over a thousand miles. Her bravery helped later space travelers.

   _____

3. Life can be hard for young birds. They may be eaten by animals. They may fall out of their nests and break their necks. But rain is the worst problem for baby birds. When it rains, grown-up birds have a hard time finding food. They stay away from the nest for longer. The baby birds in the nest may freeze in the rain.

   _____

4. One of the widest and oldest trees in the world is in Mexico. It is a giant cypress tree. It stands in front of a church. It is so big that it takes forty children to make a ring around it. Some scientists think the tree is five thousand years old.

   _____

5. Most people agree that driving makes life easier. An odd Nebraska law once made driving a chore. In the early 1900s, the state passed a law. The law was in effect at night on country roads. Each driver had to send up a skyrocket every 150 yards. It was to warn that a car was coming. After shooting the rocket, drivers had to wait eight minutes. That was to let people and animals get out of the way. Then the car could keep going.

   _____

C ▶ Apply

In your own words, state the main idea of each passage.

1. People don't talk just with words. Our faces and our clothes say things about us. So does the way we move. Animals also send messages in many ways. Not only do they make sounds. Their color, smell, and bodies speak clearly. Bees talk about food by the way they move. They do a dance. It tells other bees where to find food. Whales "talk" with lovely songs. The songs travel well under water.

   _____

   _____

2. Most animals with backbones also have a tail. Some animals use their tails as an extra arm. Monkeys use their tails to keep them steady in trees. Cows use their tails to swat flies. A fish uses its tail to swim. Foxes put their bushy tails on their paws and noses at night. This keeps them warm.

   _____

   _____

3. The cry of a wolf sounds lonely. But wolves are really calling to other wolves. Wolves have strong family ties. Many mate for life. Both parents care for their pups. Most wolf packs are family groups. They help each other find food and shelter. Their howls and calls keep the pack together.

   _____

   _____

4. An orchestra is made up of many musicians. They play four main types of instruments. One group of instruments is the strings, such as violins. There is a section called brass. It includes the horns and trumpets. Flutes and oboes are woodwinds. The percussion section has drums and chimes.

   _____

   _____

Read each passage. Circle the answer for each question.

Birds often bathe in water. But sometimes they take a dust bath. A dust bath can really help a bird. Birds have oil in their feathers. It helps keep water off them. But too much oil isn't good. It makes it harder for a bird to fly. So birds roll around in the dust. The dust soaks up the extra oil. Then the birds brush off the dust.

1. What is the main idea of this passage?

   A Birds take baths in water.

   B There are many different kinds of birds.

   C Oil is bad for birds.

   D Birds sometimes take dust baths.

Some of today's trains are built under the ground. They travel through tunnels called tubes. It is the one way to escape the traffic on the roads. The largest subway is in London. It is 220 feet deep. The tubes run for 252 miles. The world's busiest subway is in New York City. Over two billion people ride on the trains each year.

2. This passage is mainly about

   F London

   G train tunnels

   H subways

   J city traffic

In ancient Rome, soldiers were paid in salt. Salt was valuable. Soldiers could trade the salt for food and a place to live. Their pay was called "salt money." The Latin word for salt is *salarium*. After a time, the soldiers were no longer paid in salt. But they still called the money they earned a *salarium*. And that's where we get the word *salary*—the money people earn for work.

3. What is the main idea of this passage?

   A Roman soldiers used salt wisely.

   B Salt was valued in ancient times.

   C The word *salary* comes from ancient Rome.

   D Words come from many different places.

Comparing and Contrasting

One way writers explain a topic is to compare or contrast parts of the topic. When you compare, you tell how the things are alike. When you contrast, you tell how things are different.

Some plants are grown because they are useful. People make food, cloth, wood, and dyes from these plants. On the other hand, some plants are grown just because they are pretty. People have planted flower gardens for thousands of years.

This passage talks about two different groups of plants. The first two sentences have details about useful plants. The last two sentences have details about pretty plants. Find the words *on the other hand*. The words show that the second part is different from the first.

Read the passage and answer the questions.

People have two kinds of joints in their bodies. These are joints that can move and joints that can't. The first kind hold movable parts of the body together. These include the joints in arms and legs. Fixed joints are deeper inside the body. They hold the ribs together. They keep the skull in one piece. They are hard to break. Movable joints are easier to break.

1. In what way are both kinds of joints alike?

   A They are hard to break.

   B They are in the legs.

   C They hold parts of the body together.

   D The passage does not tell how they are alike.

2. What is one way the two kinds of joints differ?

   F They connect parts of the body.

   G They are found in people's bodies.

   H They are fixed or movable.

   J They hold other body parts together.

Read the passage. Write the answers to the questions.

Have you ever heard of a kangaroo rat? How about a rat kangaroo? They are two different animals. Both are about a foot long. Both hop on long back legs. Both have a head like a rat and a long tail. But the kangaroo rat has some white fur. The rat kangaroo is brown all over. Kangaroo rats don't drink water. But rat kangaroos do need water. Kangaroo rats live only in North America. Rat kangaroos live in Australia. The biggest difference of all is that the rat kangaroo has a pouch. The kangaroo rat does not.

1. What two things does the passage compare and contrast?

   _____

2. What is one way that the rat kangaroo and the kangaroo rat are alike?

   _____

3. What word is used to signal likenesses at the beginning of three sentences?

   _____

4. What word is used to signal a contrast at the beginning of two sentences?

   _____

5. What is the biggest difference between the two animals?

   _____

 **Apply**

Read the passage. Then complete the chart to show likenesses and differences.

In some ways, plants and animals are alike. They are both alive. They both grow. They both respond to light and water. But it is easy to see that there are big differences. For example, animals respond more to the world around them. Plants respond very slowly. They can turn their leaves to the light, but it may take all day. Animals are not rooted to one spot. They can roam the fields and forests. While they are roaming, they can find food. They eat solid food. Plants make their own food.

Plants and Animals

Likenesses	Differences

D▸ Check Up

Read the passage. Circle the answer for each question.

It's hard to tell rabbits and hares apart. The names are no help. For example, the jackrabbit is really a hare. Hares are larger than rabbits. They have longer ears. Hares have longer and stronger legs than rabbits. Hares live above the ground in bushes or tree stumps. Rabbits live in burrows. When hares are born, they have open eyes and a full coat of fur. But rabbits are born furless. Their eyes are closed. They need lots of care from their mothers.

1. What is the main subject being compared and contrasted?

   A rabbits and jackrabbits

   B bushes and burrows

   C rabbits and hares

   D baby rabbits and baby hares

2. The words *larger, longer,* and *stronger* are used to

   F show likenesses

   G show differences

   H introduce a new topic

   J conclude the passage

3. How is the paragraph organized?

   A The first half is about one topic. The second half is about the other.

   B The details of the two topics are discussed one at a time.

   C Time order is used.

   D There is no organization.

4. What is the main way rabbits and hares are alike?

   F They look alike.

   G They have the same homes.

   H They eat the same things.

   J They are alike as babies.

5. In the third sentence, the words *For example* are used to

   A signal a difference

   B signal a likeness

   C introduce the topic

   D introduce a detail

A ▶ Introduce

Comparing and Contrasting

What if you wanted to tell facts about tulips and roses? One way would be to compare and contrast them. To compare the flowers, you would tell how they are alike. To contrast them, you would tell how they differ.

Read the passage. Then circle the answers to the questions.

Rain forest animals include monkeys. Animals that live in open spaces include elephants. Jungle animals are different from animals that live in open spaces. Jungle animals do not see as well. That is because they don't need to see far in the jungle. They don't need a good sense of smell either. That is because there is not much wind in the jungle. Wind carries smells. Jungle animals have good hearing. They listen closely in the dark woods. A monkey can hear an enemy long before it sees it. That gives the monkey time to hide.

1. What are the main things contrasted in the passage?

   A monkeys and jungle animals

   B jungle animals and animals that live in the open

   C jungles and open spaces

   D smelling and hearing

2. How does the sight of jungle animals compare to that of other animals?

   F It is better.

   G It is just as good.

   H It works differently.

   J It is not as good.

3. Why is a good sense of smell not as important in the jungle as in open spaces?

   A There are no smells in the jungle.

   B There's little wind to carry smells in the jungle.

   C Too much wind blows smells away too quickly.

   D Too many things in the jungle smell alike.

◆B◆ Practice

Read the passage. Then write the answers to the questions.

Comets and meteors are both bodies in space. They look alike to most people. Both are bright white. But they are white for different reasons. The white of a meteor comes from heat. The white of a comet comes from reflected light. Meteors are chunks of metal. They heat up as they fall through the earth's atmosphere. Most meteors burn up before reaching the ground. On the other hand, comets do not fall to the earth. They stay in space. The ice and dust of a comet reflect light from the sun.

1. What two things does the passage compare and contrast?

   _____

2. In what way do comets and meteors look alike?

   _____

3. How is the light of comets and meteors different?

   _____

   _____

4. Name one other way comets and meteors differ.

   _____

   _____

5. What group of words is used to signal a difference between comets and meteors?

   _____

   _____

C ▶ Apply

Read the passage. Then complete the chart.

Dolphins are mammals. Marine dolphins live in salt water. They can be found in most of the world's oceans. But some dolphins don't live in the ocean. River dolphins live in freshwater. They live in rivers in South America and Asia. The adults are about five to eight feet long. On the other hand, marine dolphins may be up to thirty feet long. The snout of a river dolphin is about one foot long. The snout of a marine dolphin is one-fourth that size. Marine dolphins see well. But river dolphins have very small eyes. They are almost blind. Like marine dolphins, river dolphins are warm-blooded. They eat fish and shellfish like marine dolphins. But river dolphins find their food by rooting through the mud at the bottom of the river.

	Marine Dolphins	**River Dolphins**
Fish or Mammal?		
Home		
Snout		
Size		
Food		
Sight		

Read the passage. Then circle the answers to the questions.

The kiwi is a rare bird. Unlike most birds, the kiwi has a keen sense of smell. Most birds have nostrils at the base of their beaks. But the kiwi's nostrils are at the end of its bill. Another unusual thing about the kiwi is its brown feathers. They look and feel like hair. The kiwi also has hairs near its bill. They look like whiskers. Like a cat, a kiwi uses the whiskers to find its way in the dark. The strangest thing is that the kiwi does not fly. It runs fast.

1. What is the main thing the kiwi is compared and contrasted to?

   A hair

   B fruit

   C cats

   D other birds

2. In the first sentence, the word *rare* means

   F unusual

   G not well cooked

   H very valuable

   J sick

3. The kiwi's feathers are different from those of other birds because

   A they are brown

   B they are like hair

   C they are soft

   D they are near its bill

4. The main differences between kiwis and other birds are

   F where they live

   G what they eat

   H how they look and act

   J how they sound

5. What can you learn about other birds from the passage?

   A They have whiskers.

   B They are like cats.

   C They have brown feathers.

   D They do not have a good sense of smell.

Read On Read "All Kinds of Cats." Answer the questions and look for comparisons and contrasts in the article.

 **Introduce**

Drawing Conclusions

Sometimes a passage may contain ideas that are not stated directly. Then you must draw a conclusion. When you do this, you decide what facts mean.

Dogs can be trained to do many things. Some kinds of dogs are guides for blind people. Others find people who are lost in mountains. Farm dogs herd cattle.

This passage tells some details about dogs. What can you conclude after reading the details? You might conclude that *dogs are smart animals*. The details support this conclusion.

Read the passage. Then circle the correct answers.

How was coffee discovered? An old story tells how. It says that a boy who herded goats first tried coffee. His goats ate some red berries from a certain tree. The goats became very active. So the goatherd ate some. He felt more awake. People soon found the best way to dry and grind the coffee beans from the coffee tree.

1. From the passage we can conclude that when coffee was discovered,
   A people were afraid of its effects
   B people were glad to find a way to stay awake
   C people had many ways to feel more awake
   D people did not like to try new things

2. What can we conclude about the part of coffee that keeps people awake?
   F It is natural.
   G It is added at the store.
   H It has no real effect on people.
   J It is dangerous.

3. What can we conclude about discovering new foods and drinks?
   A Most are discovered by scientists.
   B Often they are discovered by goatherds.
   C They were all discovered a very long time ago.
   D They may be discovered by accident.

Read each passage. Then read the conclusion drawn from the facts. Decide whether the conclusion is a good one based on the facts. If it is, write *good conclusion* on the line. If it is not, write a conclusion that is reasonable.

1. Origami is the art of paper folding. It is an old Japanese skill. People can make birds, flowers, and many other shapes from folded paper. From Japan, origami has spread to the West. All around the globe, paper folding is thought of as a skill, an art, or just plain fun.

   Conclusion: It is very difficult to learn origami.

   _____

2. There are thousands of kinds of seashells. They are found all over the world. Some are as small as peas. The giant clam shell, though, is very big. It can be up to three feet wide. Over the years, shells have been used many different ways. They have been used as tools, money, spoons, and dishes.

   Conclusion: Shells come in all shapes and sizes.

   _____

3. Ambrose Burnside was an army general. He fought for the Union Army in the Civil War. He had no beard. But he grew short whiskers down the sides of his face. They covered parts of his cheeks. Soon other men began to grow whiskers like Burnside's. At first they called them "burnsides." Soon the name was changed to "sideburns."

   Conclusion: Burnside must have been disliked by the men in the army.

   _____

4. The blue moonwort bores through ice. Believe it or not, the blue moonwort is a plant. It lives in the Swiss Alps. It is very cold there. The moonwort is buried by snow all winter. In spring, it sprouts buds. The buds give off a little heat. The heat softens the ice. The moonwort stem pushes up. Finally the flower cracks through the top layer of ice.

   Conclusion: The moonwort can live in colder areas than most flowers.

   _____

C Apply

Read each passage. Then write an answer to each question.

1. Butterflies drink from a built-in straw. A butterfly has no mouth. It can't chew. So it eats with a long, thin tube. Through the tube, the butterfly can suck up sweet nectar.

   What can you conclude about the kinds of food a butterfly eats?

   _____

2. An actor named Tom London holds a record. He was in more films than any other actor. He first appeared in *The Great Train Robbery* in 1919. He played a train driver. That was his job in real life. Soon he got many leading roles. Then he played character roles. He often played the sheriff in Westerns. By 1959, he had been in two thousand movies.

   What can you conclude about Tom London's skill as an actor?

   _____

3. Frost harms crops. But it also does some good. Some trees start to grow too much fruit. One or two frosts in the spring can harm the tree. They can kill much of a tree's blossoms. Then the tree's strength goes to make less fruit. But the fruit is better.

   What might happen to the fruit from trees if there were no frosts?

   _____

4. A greenhouse is not green. It is clear. That is because it is made of glass. The glass lets in the sun's heat. That helps plants grow. The green plants are the reason for the name. They grow all year round in the warm, sunny room.

   What can you conclude that plants need to grow?

   _____

D ▶ Check Up

Read the passage. Circle the answer for each question.

Scientists start with small bits of information. They try to piece them together. They try to understand what they mean. They want to know the whole story. Some scientists work with fossils. These are scraps of ancient life. They may be old bones, imprints of plants in stone, or the hardened remains of other living things. They hold clues to the past. Scientists have been studying fossils for a hundred years. They have found out much about life on Earth millions of years ago. Maybe someday the picture will be complete.

1. We can conclude that being a scientist is like being

   A a factory worker

   B an ancient fossil

   C a detective

   D a painter

2. We can conclude that fossils

   F are very valuable to scientists

   G are easy to find

   H are easy to understand

   J were purposely left by ancient people

3. We can conclude that

   A scientists will figure out the whole picture of life on Earth very soon

   B scientists will keep working with fossils

   C scientists' work with fossils has not been useful

   D scientists won't learn anything new from fossils in the future

4. We can conclude that fossils

   F are very old things made by people

   G are only the remains of animals

   H are only the remains of ancient plants

   J are the remains of all kinds of ancient life

Drawing Conclusions

When you draw a conclusion, you decide what facts mean. You figure out the ideas that are not directly stated. When you draw a conclusion, make sure it is supported by the facts. What conclusions can you draw from the passage below?

Would you stand in line for five years? Believe it or not, you will. Standing in line is part of life. Experts say that a person stands in line for a total of five years.

Suppose you concluded that standing in line is good for you. This is a faulty conclusion. The facts do not support it. But you can conclude that everyone has to stand in line sometimes.

Read the passage. Then circle the answers to the questions.

Once all dogs were wild. No one knows who tamed them. Some people think that the first wild dogs came from wolves. Over the years, the wild dogs changed. They lost their fear of people. They let people feed them. They were soon willing to become pets.

1. We can conclude that dogs
   A found that being a pet was easier than being wild
   B were all wolves, and now there are no wolves
   C did not like to be given food
   D did not like attention from people

2. We can conclude that the change in dogs
   F happened very quickly
   G took hundreds or thousands of years
   H could be reversed in the future
   J was expected

3. What can we conclude about people's feelings about dogs?
   A They have changed recently.
   B People have always feared dogs.
   C People have never liked dogs.
   D People have liked dogs for a long time.

B Practice

Read each passage. Then read the conclusion based on the passage. If the conclusion is supported by the facts, write *valid*. If it is not, write a new conclusion.

1. People sweat. Dogs and cats pant. These are both ways to release heat. Birds have a different way. They are very active. So they build up a lot of heat. When they fly, they breathe a lot of air. They use half the air to cool their bodies.

   Conclusion: Animals keep cool in different ways.

   _____

2. Who was the first person to reach the North Pole? No one can say for sure. Yet a few explorers have made claims. One was Frederick Cook. He headed to the Pole in 1908. It took him a long time to return. When he did, he said he had reached the North Pole. But another explorer, Robert Peary, made his own claim. He said he had been at the North Pole at the same time. He didn't know about Cook's claim. In 1926 Richard Byrd said he flew over the Pole. That claim could not be proven, either.

   Conclusion: Early explorers of the North Pole were all fakes.

   _____

3. Some people hate spiders. But spiders help us. They eat bugs day and night. There are millions and millions of insects on Earth. What if spiders did not eat bugs? The bugs would eat all of our crops.

   Conclusion: If spiders suddenly disappeared, we would starve to death.

   _____

4. People eat a lot of grass. They do not eat lawn grass, though. Most grains are types of grasses. Oats, barley, corn, and wheat are types of grass. Cereal and bread are made from grasses. These grains have lots of vitamins and fiber. Grasses can be sweet too. Most of the sugar we eat comes from sugar cane. Sugar cane is a type of grass.

   Conclusion: Grasses are not good for people to eat.

   _____

C ▸ Apply

Read each passage. Then write an answer to each question.

1. A line of wet clothes led to the first hot-air balloon. In France in 1782, a woman hung her clothes out to dry. She built a small fire under them. She wanted them to dry faster. All at once her skirt filled with hot air from the fire. It began to rise. Her husband saw this happen. He tried filling a balloon with hot air. Soon he made a trip in a balloon over Paris.

   What can you conclude about what hot air does?

   _____

   _____

2. Where would you go to see a desert? You could try the Middle East. There are deserts in Egypt and other places in the Middle East. It is hot and dry there. You could go to the southwestern United States. There are large deserts there. You could also go to Alaska. People think of this state as being snowy and icy. But there is a desert there too. It has high sand dunes. It is often freezing there. But, like deserts in Egypt and America, it is very dry.

   What can you conclude about how all deserts are alike?

   _____

   _____

3. The old country of Persia used to have princes. The children of the princes had many teachers. They got their first teachers when they were babies. At age seven, the children learned to ride a horse. At fourteen, they began learning from wise priests. One priest taught the value of truth. Another taught courage. Another taught the children how to control their emotions.

   What can you conclude about the schooling of royal children in Persia?

   _____

   _____

Read each passage. Then circle the answer for each question.

People started using zippers in 1891. Whitcomb L. Judson was a Chicago inventor. In his day, shoes were hooked with buttons. He made a zipper for shoes. He wanted to make them easier to hook. But the zipper was used in other ways instead. Judson's invention ended up changing the way clothes were made.

1. We can conclude that people
   A did not think the zipper was useful
   B had no need for Judson's invention
   C saw that the zipper could be used in more ways than one
   D did not understand how the zipper worked

2. We can conclude that Judson
   F was not smart
   G made a successful invention
   H was upset about how people used the zipper
   J made no money from the zipper

3. The story of Judson's zipper shows that
   A people don't need new ways of doing things
   B people don't respect inventors
   C shoes should be buttoned and not zipped
   D there is always room for new ways of doing things

4. We can conclude that zippers
   F were invented before buttons
   G made buttons useless
   H gave people a different way to fasten clothes
   J were more useful than buttons

Drawing Conclusions

Reading the facts in a passage is the first step in reading. But it is not enough. You need to figure out what the facts mean. You need to see the whole picture. When you do this, you are drawing a conclusion. When you draw a conclusion, use all the facts. A conclusion that makes sense based on all the facts is a *valid* conclusion. A conclusion that does not make sense based on the facts is an *invalid* conclusion.

Read the passage below. Then circle the answers to the questions.

Some heroes save lives. Others do hard jobs that most people won't try. John "Snowshoe" Thompson lived in the 1800s. John went West to look for gold. He never found any. But he was a good skier. He decided to take mail over the mountains of the West. People thought he would not live through the first winter. But John carried the mail for fifteen years.

1. What can we conclude about John Thompson?

   A He was a failure because he didn't find gold.

   B He was tough and brave.

   C He settled for a boring job.

   D He was afraid to try new things.

2. The route that John traveled must have been

   F covered with wild animals

   G hot, dry desert

   H cold and dangerous

   J well traveled

3. John Thompson was a hero because he

   A saved people's lives

   B did a hard job for many years

   C lived in the West

   D was not good at his job

B ▶ Practice

Read each passage. Decide whether the conclusion is valid or not. If it is, write *valid*. If it is not, write *invalid*.

1. Three hundred years ago, combs cost a lot of money. When pirates robbed people on ships, they would take their combs. Combs from nine hundred years ago were made of bone. Later, combs made of gold were used in church. They were used to comb the priest's hair. In Japan, some people do not like to throw away a comb. They think it is bad luck.

   Conclusion: People have always thought that combs brought good luck.

   _____

2. When Columbus came to America, there were hundreds of American Indian groups. They had their own languages. They made tools of stone and metal. Some were good farmers. Others made silver and gold jewelry.

   Conclusion: Long before Europeans came to America, American Indians had rich and differing ways of life.

   _____

3. "Ike" Eisenhower was a famous general. He was president of the United States for two terms. Jim Thorpe was one of the greatest athletes in history. He was an Olympic track champion. He also played baseball and football. One day these two men met on the football field. Ike played for West Point. In one play, he tried to tackle Thorpe. Thorpe was not hurt. But Ike had to leave the game. He had hurt his knee.

   Conclusion: Ike Eisenhower was not a good football player.

   _____

4. A *browse* is a twig from a tree or shrub. Sometimes animals walk along and nibble at these things. They are said to be browsing. A while back, people began to use the word for people. They said that people who just nibbled on food were browsing. Then the word was used for shoppers. Some people looked in stores but did not buy. They were called browsers.

   Conclusion: People should not look at things that they are not going to buy.

   _____

C ▶ Apply

Read each passage. Then write an answer to each question.

An elephant baby is weak when it is born. Its legs wobble. It cannot control its trunk. The mother is not the only one that cares for the baby. So does the leader of the herd. So do aunts and older sisters.

1. What conclusion can you draw about elephant families?

_____

_____

The highest mountain in Peru is Huascaran. Annie Peck wanted to be the first person to climb it. She began climbing mountains when she was forty-five years old. In 1908 she was in her late fifties. Annie and two guides started climbing Huascaran. The guides got sick. They turned back. Ten days later, Annie and the group began climbing again. She and her guides faced bitter cold and strong winds. But they made it to the top. Annie and the guides were was the first people to climb the mountain.

2. What conclusion can you draw about Annie Peck's character?

_____

_____

Old English houses had narrow openings. They let in the light. But they also let the wind in. So people called them "wind eyes." In 1238, King Henry III got tired of the wind in his palace. He had glass put over the wind eyes. No wind could get in. But people kept calling them "wind eyes." Soon the way people said the words changed. Today we call these openings "windows."

3. What can you conclude about how some words form?

_____

_____

◆D▶ Check Up

Read the passage. Then circle the answers to the questions.

Some hunters use a pack of dogs to hunt foxes. Foxes use many tricks to fool the dogs. A fox may retrace its steps. Then it will make a long jump to the side. The dogs will go where they thought the fox was headed. A fox may walk along the top of a fence. Or it may hide among some cows. Both these tricks hide the scent of the fox. Sometimes a fox makes friends with the dogs. Then the dogs will not lead the hunters to the fox.

1. We can conclude that dogs track foxes by

   A following hunters

   B a process that people don't understand

   C using sight or smell

   D knowing a fox's habits

2. We can conclude that hunters use dogs to hunt foxes because

   F dogs can often find a fox

   G foxes use tricks to fool dogs

   H they don't want to find the foxes

   J they think foxes are smarter than dogs

3. The passage shows that the fox is

   A smarter than the dog

   B easily fooled

   C a shy, slow animal

   D easy to hunt

4. From this passage, we can conclude that

   F dogs are always used to hunt foxes

   G people hunt foxes for many reasons

   H foxes have learned many ways to avoid hunters

   J foxes are hunted in the summertime

Recognizing Cause and Effect

How many times a day do you ask *Why?* When you ask why, you want to know the *cause* of something. Something that happens for a reason is an *effect*. For example, think about a person getting a sunburn. The *cause* of the sunburn was being out in the sun too long. A sunburn was an *effect* of staying in the sun.

Read the passage. Circle the correct answers.

Chances are you have never seen a California condor. These giant birds may be dying out forever. Scientists think there are fewer than thirty left on Earth. People have used more and more land for farms, roads, and cities. This land has been taken away from animals. Some of the birds died from poisons. Farmers were using the poisons to kill other animals. Condors are now protected.

1. Why will you probably never see a California condor?

   A The birds live in South America.

   B The birds hide from people.

   C The birds are dying out quickly.

   D The birds are very small.

2. What was the cause of the condor dying out?

   F People killed the birds for sport.

   G People took over the land where the birds lived.

   H Farmers tried to kill the birds.

   J People started protecting the birds.

3. People realized that condors were dying out. What was the effect of this?

   A They started protecting the birds.

   B They decided the birds were useless.

   C They kept taking land away from the birds.

   D They built more cities.

Read each sentence. Then write the cause or effect described in the sentence.

1. Because he liked to dress in fancy clothes, the prince Mir Bahboob Ali Khan wore a different outfit every day.

   Cause: _____

   _____

   Effect: The prince wore a different outfit every day.

2. Ferns and mosses grow well on the forest floor because they do not need much light.

   Cause: Ferns and mosses do not need much light.

   Effect: _____

   _____

3. Your eyes have tears at all times because if your eyes got dry, you'd go blind.

   Cause: Without tears you would go blind.

   Effect: _____

   _____

4. People and animals have hair because it gives them warmth and protection.

   Cause: _____

   _____

   Effect: People and animals have hair.

C ▶ Apply

Read the passages. Then write the answers to the questions.

There are people who live as people in the Stone Age did. The natives of Australia live close to nature. They have no homes. They roam their land. They eat kangaroo, lizards, nuts, and ants. This is a good diet for them. The people get a lot of fresh air and exercise. The hot climate keeps them from getting sick much. These people live long. They are rarely sick.

1. Write three reasons why the natives of Australia live long and rarely get sick.

_____

_____

_____

2. Why do you think the natives of Australia eat kangaroo, lizards, nuts, and ants?

_____

_____

Day and night, ocean waves wash against the shore. The waves have been coming in for millions of years. In fact, the waves made the sand on the beach. The sand was once sharp rocks, pebbles, and shells. The waves carried them back and forth, back and forth. Slowly the waves ground the shells and rocks into tiny bits.

3. Why are beaches filled with sand?

_____

_____

4. What would beaches be like if the ocean sat still instead of rolling onto the land in waves?

_____

_____

Read the passages. Then circle the correct answers.

Wind is caused by the sun. Here's how it works. The sun does not heat the air evenly. The air is warmest close to the earth. Farther away from the earth, the air is cooler. Warm air rises. When it does, the cool air sinks and takes its place. Then that cool air is warmed, and it rises. This flow goes on and on. The flow creates wind.

1. What is the effect of warm air and cool air changing places?

   A sunlight

   B warmth

   C wind

   D heated air

2. The sun causes wind because

   F it makes clouds

   G it heats up trees

   H it makes cool air sink

   J it makes unevenly heated air

Ergs are found in deserts. They are also called sand seas. They are big areas of loose sand. Strong winds blow the sand, resulting in sandstorms. These sandstorms make it very hard to travel across ergs. The ergs of the Sahara Desert are the worst in the world.

3. Why are ergs hard to travel across?

   A They are in deserts.

   B They have sand.

   C They are called sand seas.

   D They have many sandstorms.

4. What causes sandstorms?

   F ergs

   G winds

   H sand seas

   J the deserts

Understanding Cause and Effect

When you read, look for passages that tell about cause and effect. Look for words like *so, therefore,* and *because.* These show cause and effect in sentences.

> People thought four-leaf clovers were lucky because they were rare.

In this sentence, the word *because* signals cause and effect. The *effect* is that people thought four-leaf clovers were lucky. The *cause* is that the clovers are rare.

Read the passage. Circle the correct answers.

> The "screech" owl is not well named. The owl's sound is not a screech. Some people think it sounds like the whinny of a colt. But young owls make a different sound. They hum. Then their parents feed them. They hum until they are full. When they stop humming, their parents stop feeding them. When they hum again, the parent owls feed them again.

1. Why do young screech owls hum?

    A because they want to sound like their parents

    B because they are tired

    C because they are full

    D because they are hungry

2. What is the effect when a baby owl stops humming?

    F The parents feed it.

    G The parents stop feeding it.

    H The owl learns to screech.

    J The parents think it is sick.

3. Why is a "screech" owl not well named?

    A because baby owls hum

    B because the owls don't make sounds

    C because the owls don't make a screeching sound

    D because only colts screech

Each sentence is followed by a cause or an effect. If the cause is stated, write the effect. If the effect is stated, write the cause.

1. In the 1500s tulips were very valuable because they were rare.

   Cause: _____

   _____

   Effect: Tulips were valuable.

2. Fish swim in large groups so they can protect each other.

   Cause: Fish need to protect each other.

   Effect: _____

   _____

3. Long ago people took few baths because bath water had to be brought from wells in town.

   Cause: Water had to be brought from town.

   Effect: _____

   _____

4. Owls are good at catching prey at night because they see well in the dark.

   Cause: _____

   _____

   Effect: Owls catch prey well at night.

5. Hunters hide behind tall grass so that game birds can't see them.

   Cause: Hunters hide behind grass.

   Effect: _____

   _____

C ◆ Apply

Read each passage. Write the answers to the questions.

A kind of woodpecker is in trouble. It is the red-cockaded woodpecker. It nests in big pine forests. It nests only in trees that are at least forty years old. That is because the center of the trunk must be rotten. Then the bird's nest will be soft. Today, there are fewer than ten thousand of these birds left. That is because people cut down older pine forests. They cut them down for wood.

1. Why does the woodpecker nest in older trees?

_____

2. Why is the woodpecker in trouble?

_____

3. Why have people cut down pine forests?

_____

One early group of human beings was the Neanderthals. Their world was much simpler than ours. They had to make their own tools. One tool was a sharp stick. They used the sticks to hunt and dig. The Neanderthals had better stick tools than other groups. That is because they had made stone knives. They could sharpen the sticks with the knives.

4. Why did Neanderthals use sharp sticks?

_____

5. Why were the sticks of the Neanderthals better than some others?

_____

Read the passages. Circle the answer to each question.

The first humans in North America got there by walking. They crossed the Bering Sea from Asia. The sea was frozen then. It was during the Great Ice Age. It was about twenty-five thousand years ago. The people were hunters. They made the trip because they were following a wild herd. After a while, the earth grew warmer. The Bering Sea thawed.

1. Why did people first walk from Asia to North America?

    A They were explorers.

    B They were running away from the Ice Age.

    C They were following animals that they hunted.

    D They were looking for a warmer climate.

2. Why do people not walk from Asia to North America today?

    F People are no longer hunters.

    G The Bering Sea between the continents is water.

    H They do not need to.

    J There are no more wild herds.

Because they are tall, giraffes serve as lookouts. They can see very well. A giraffe may see an enemy far away. Then it will warn the rest of the herd. The herd runs to escape the enemy. Herds of other animals run too.

3. Why do giraffes serve as lookouts?

    A They have good sense of smell.

    B They are tall.

    C They warn the herd.

    D They run fast.

4. What causes the lookouts to warn the rest of the herd?

    F An enemy appears.

    G The giraffes begin running.

    H Other herds are running.

    J They can see well.

A ▸ Introduce

Understanding Cause and Effect

Sometimes people write to tell why something happens. They may explain why birds sing. They may tell why the color of the ocean changes. When you tell why something happens, you explore causes and effects. Causes are the reasons for events. Effects are the result of these causes.

Read the first sentence. Then complete the second sentence with the word *cause* **or the word** *effect.*

1. Ocean birds build nests on the shore because they find their food at sea.

   The place where ocean birds live is the _____ of their food choice.

2. Rattlesnakes crawl into sleeping bags to get warm at night.

   Being cold is the _____ of snakes crawling into sleeping bags at night.

3. The pupils of your eyes get smaller when you are in bright light.

   Bright light is the _____ of your pupils getting smaller.

4. Poodles are used in the circus because they learn tricks quickly.

   For poodles, being in the circus is the _____ of learning tricks quickly.

5. People used the saying "learning by heart" because they believed people thought with their hearts.

   A wrong idea about the heart was the _____ of the phrase "learning by heart."

B ▶ Practice

Read each passage. Then write the answers to the questions.

In ancient Greek myth, Pan was the god of woods and fields. He watched over shepherds and sheep. He was half man and half goat. He played music on pipes. The pipes were made from reeds. People thought any odd sounds at night were made by Pan. In fact, the word *panic* comes from the word *Pan*. *Panic* means "sudden fear."

1. Why did people name the word for "sudden fear" after Pan?

_____

_____

Have you ever seen a cat's eyes at night? They shine in the dark. A cat hunts at night. How can shining eyes help a night hunter? They help it see better in the dark. In daylight, the cat's pupils get tiny. In the dark, they open wide. Lots of light can enter. The back of the cat's eyes are like a mirror. It reflects all the light. Some of the light shines back at you.

2. What is the cause of a cat's eyes shining in the dark?

_____

_____

If you ever get lost in the woods, go to a tree. It can help you find your way out. Trees grow in ways that show north and south. For example, leaves are thicker on the south side of a tree. The top of a tree bends to the south. The color of bark is lighter on the south side. On the other hand, moss grows on the north side of a tree.

3. Why should you look at a tree if you get lost in the woods?

_____

_____

C ▸ Apply

Read the passage. Complete the chart.

You don't see many pots and pans with metal handles. There's a good reason for that. Metal gets hot very quickly. Try leaving a metal spoon in a bowl of hot soup. The spoon will get as hot as the soup. The heat from the soup flows into the spoon. Metal is a good thing to use for a frying pan. It gets hot and stays hot. But the heat from the stove would heat a metal handle too. Wood and plastic would not make good pans. They don't conduct heat well. But they are good for handles for that reason.

CAUSE	EFFECT
1.	A metal spoon in a bowl of hot soup gets hot.
2.	Metal makes good frying pans.
3.	Plastic is good for pan handles.
4.	Metal is not good for pan handles.
5.	Wood is not a good material for a pan.

D Check Up

Read the passage. Circle the answers to the questions.

Porpoises sleep with one eye open. This is so they don't drown in their sleep. Porpoises are mammals so they need to breathe air. They come out of the water now and then to breathe. They do this even in their sleep. But the water can be rough. The dolphins may take in water. So they sleep with an eye open. Then they can check the size of the waves.

1. Why do porpoises need to breathe air?

   A because they live in the sea

   B because they are land animals

   C because they are mammals

   D because they sleep in rough water

2. Why can sleeping be dangerous for porpoises?

   F because they may take in water in rough seas

   G because they can't jump out of the water in their sleep

   H because they can't breathe

   J because they may get attacked

3. What is the effect of the danger to porpoises?

   A They don't breathe at night.

   B They don't sleep.

   C They sleep during the day.

   D They keep an eye open when they sleep.

4. Why do porpoises come out of the water now and then?

   F to sleep

   G to swim

   H to avoid enemies

   J to breathe

Read On Read "The Great Depression." Answer the questions and look for cause-and-effect relationships in the article.

A Introduce

Summarizing and Paraphrasing

One good way to understand what you read is to **summarize** it. When you summarize a passage, you tell its main ideas. You leave out most of the details. So a **summary** is much shorter than the original passage.

Sometimes, you may decide to **paraphrase** a passage instead of summarizing it. When you paraphrase, you put a sentence or a paragraph into your own words. A paraphrase may be about as long as the original. But it will be in simpler words. Like a summary, a paraphrase helps you understand what you read. When you summarize or paraphrase, be sure to include all the important ideas.

Read the passage. Answer each question.

In A.D. 55, what is now England was taken by the Romans. The Celts lived there. They became slaves to the Romans. Before the Romans came, the Celts lived in huts. They could not read or write. The Romans taught them to build houses of stone and brick. The Romans built schools. They taught the Celts to read and write Latin.

1. What is the best summary of the passage?

    A The Celts became slaves of the Romans in A.D. 55.

    B The Celts lived in huts.

    C The Romans brought stone houses and education to the Celts.

    D The Celts learned to read and write Latin.

2. Paraphrase the passage.

    _____

    _____

    _____

    _____

B Practice

Write a paraphrase of each passage.

1. Not all wild animals are strong and mean. Many are small and weak. But that doesn't mean they are helpless. They develop other skills to help them live.

   _____

   _____

2. Bald eagles are not really bald. Their heads are covered with feathers. Most of the eagle's feathers are dark brown. But its head feathers are white. The white feathers make the eagle look bald from far away.

   _____

   _____

3. Rainbows don't appear only when the sun shines. Moonlight can also make a rainbow. It's called a moonbow. It may appear after a night rain. The moon must be very bright for a moonbow to show up.

   _____

   _____

4. Hundreds of years ago, kings had jesters. The job of jesters was to act like clowns. They wore bright costumes and caps with bells on them.

   _____

   _____

5. The Milky Way is full of stars and planets. But how can you tell the difference between them? A star is a large ball of glowing gases. Planets are dark, solid bodies. They are much smaller than stars.

   _____

   _____

C Apply

Write a summary of each passage.

1. For many years, oil and gas have been our main fuels. Coal used to be the most important fuel. But the world's supply of coal, oil, and gas is limited. Those fuels took millions of years to form. They formed in the earth. Once they are gone, they are gone forever. So scientists are trying to find and make new fuels.

   _____

   _____

2. The sun gives off energy all the time. The energy has been pretty steady for millions of years. But at times it puts out less energy. That is what caused the earth's ice ages. Less heat and light came to the earth during those times.

   _____

   _____

3. How can you measure something without a ruler? In ancient times, people used what they had on hand. Often it was a hand. It might also be a foot. The length we call a foot used to be the length of a man's foot. A hand was the width of a man's hand. A hand is still the unit used to measure horses' heights.

   _____

   _____

4. In the 1600s, the Puritans settled in New England. They made strict laws. They were called blue laws. They had many rules about what people could not do on Sundays. They could not cut their hair. Their could not make their beds. Children could not play. A mother could not kiss her child.

   _____

   _____

Read each passage. Circle the answer for each question.

In Greek stories, the three Gorgons were awful monsters. They were sisters. They had snakes on their heads instead of hair. They had flat noses and long teeth. The Greeks thought that anyone who looked at them would turn to stone.

1. Choose the best summary of the passage.

   A The three Gorgons were in Greek stories.

   B The Greeks told stories about the three Gorgons, scary sisters who could turn people to stone.

   C The Gorgons had snakes on their heads and flat noses and were monsters.

   D The Greeks made up stories.

The dragon of Komodo is a real, live creature. But it isn't really a dragon. It's the largest living lizard. The lizard looks like a dragon.

2. Choose the best paraphrase of the passage.

   F The dragon of Komodo looks real.

   G There is a lizard that looks like a dragon.

   H The largest living lizard is a dragon.

   J The dragon of Komodo is really a kind of lizard.

In the 1600s many countries in Europe traded with the East. They built big ships to carry goods. But pirates would attack the ships. They would steal the goods. So trading ships were built as warships. They had many guns.

3. Choose the best summary of the passage.

   A In the 1600s, European trading ships were built as warships to protect them from pirates.

   B Pirate ships used guns to steal from traders.

   C European ships carried many goods as they traveled east.

   D In the 1600s, pirates attacked warships and then traded the goods in the East.

Summarizing and Paraphrasing

What is one good way to understand what you read? Try putting the ideas from a passage into your own words. Sometimes you want to recall only the main ideas from a paragraph, page, or article. Then you **summarize** the ideas. A **summary** is much shorter than the original passage. Other times you may want to recall the main ideas and the details of a passage. Then you **paraphrase** the passage. A **paraphrase** may be about as long as the original. But it is in your words.

Read the passage. Then read the summary and the paraphrase of the passage.

An orchestra must have a leader. That person is called the conductor. He or she faces the orchestra. The conductor keeps time with a stick called a baton. The musicians pay close attention to the baton. It helps them all play in time. Without a leader, they would not play well together.

Summary: Every orchestra has a conductor. He or she leads the musicians with a baton.

Paraphrase: The leader of an orchestra is called the conductor. The conductor faces the musicians and waves a baton. The musicians watch the baton in order to keep time with one another.

Read the passage. Circle the answer to the question.

Plains Indians had interesting scouts. A scout would wear the skin of a wolf. It fit over his head and back. The Indians knew that buffalo did not fear wolves. So the scouts dressed as wolves. They crawled close to a herd of buffalo. Then they aimed their arrows at the big animals.

What is the best summary of the passage?

    A Plains Indians liked to dress in animal costumes.

    B Plains Indians were afraid of wolves.

    C Plains Indian scouts dressed as wolves to help them hunt buffalo.

    D Plains Indian scouts used wolf skins for luck when they hunted.

Unit 4 Constructing Meaning

B Practice

Read each passage. Then write a summary of each one.

1. Your shoe size is based on the length of barley grains. During the Middle Ages, the English king decided the length of an inch. He said it would be the size of three grains of barley. The average man's foot was thirty-nine grains long. People who made shoes called this size 13. A shoe that was three grains longer was size 14, and so on.

   _____

   _____

   _____

2. The southern tip of Africa is called the Cape of Good Hope. The cape is far south. Cold winds from the South Pole blow on it. The seas around it are rough. Explorers from Europe went around the cape to reach India. They first named it the Cape of Storms. But the king of Portugal thought the name was bad for trade. He renamed the cape. He called it the Cape of Good Hope.

   _____

   _____

   _____

3. The footprints of dinosaurs can be found near river banks. Millions of years ago, dinosaurs walked in the mud. Their feet left deep tracks. Then the sun dried the mud. The tracks filled with water, sand, and mud. After many years, the mud became rock. Many dinosaur prints have been found in the Connecticut River Valley. People can see tracks made two hundred million years ago.

   _____

   _____

   _____

C Apply

Read each passage. Then write a paraphrase of each one.

1. Weeds cause trouble for garden plants. Some weeds rob water from the soil. They don't leave any for the plants. Others grow too tall. They keep sunlight from other plants. Some weeds wrap around plants and kill them.

   _____

   _____

   _____

2. There is a famous diamond. It is three or four thousand years old. It is in the crown of the queen of England. In 1304, an Indian prince owned the gem. In the 1700s, the king of Persia owned it. He called it Kohinoor. That means "mountain of light." People believe the Kohinoor is the oldest diamond in the world.

   _____

   _____

   _____

3. Once there was a man who was king for six hours. His name was Nizam. In India in 1555, Nizam was a servant. One day he saw the king fall into the sea. He dove into the water and saved the king's life. The king was thankful. He said Nizam could be king for six hours. As king, Nizam ate a feast. He gave money to the poor. He had a special coin made.

   _____

   _____

   _____

Read each passage. Then circle the answer to each question.

Snakes would not be able to find food if it weren't for their tongues.

1. What is the best paraphrase of the sentence?

   A Snakes cannot find food.

   B Snakes do not have tongues.

   C Food isn't on the tongues of snakes.

   D Snakes use their tongues to find food.

Pigs are not stupid animals. Some pigs have been known to unlock gates and run away. And pigs never eat too much, as some animals do.

2. Choose the best paraphrase of the passage.

   F Pigs are stupid because they eat too much.

   G Pigs are not stupid. They can figure out how to escape and they do not overeat.

   H Pigs often unlock their gates and run away after eating too much.

   J Pigs are not stupid, but they do stupid things.

In the Stone Age, people got everything from the earth. They used stone, dirt, and plants to make everything. Today we still get what we need from the earth. We make glass from sand. We make plastic from oil and minerals.

3. Choose the best summary of the passage.

   A Stone Age people had few materials to make things.

   B Stone Age people used stone, dirt, and plants to make everything.

   C Like the people of the Stone Age, modern man uses things from the earth for many things.

   D People today are very different from people of the Stone Age.

Review

Characters

When you read, it helps to know what real or imaginary characters are like. A writer tells about a character in different ways. A writer may tell what the person looks like, says, or does. The writer may tell what other people think or say about the person.

Main Idea

A paragraph is a group of ideas about one main idea. The main idea links all the details in a paragraph.

Compare/Contrast

Writers often explain a topic by comparing, or telling how things are alike. They may also contrast, or tell how things are different.

Drawing Conclusions

Sometimes a passage may contain ideas that are not stated directly. You have to decide what the writer means by thinking about what was said.

Cause and Effect

When you read, you learn about some things that make other things happen. What happens is the effect, and why it happens is the cause.

Summarizing/Paraphrasing

When you summarize a passage, you tell its main ideas. When you paraphrase, you put a sentence or a paragraph into your own words. A summary is usually much shorter than a paraphrase.

Assessment

Read the paragraphs and circle the answer for each question.

Harriet Tubman had been an enslaved African American in Maryland. In 1849, she escaped to freedom with the help of the Underground Railroad. This was a group of people who helped enslaved people escape to places such as Canada where they could be free. After Tubman was free, she returned to slave states. She led hundreds of other enslaved people to their freedom. This was very dangerous, but she wanted to help free others. She became known as the Moses of her people. Moses was a person in the Bible who led the Jews out of slavery in Egypt.

1. From this paragraph, you can conclude that Tubman

   A was a very brave woman

   B was not willing to help others

   C thought only about herself

   D wanted to be called Moses

2. What is this paragraph mostly about?

   F the Underground Railroad

   G Moses

   H Egypt

   J Harriet Tubman

The Flyers and the Comets are both good baseball teams. Both teams have great pitchers. However, there are differences between the teams. The Flyers are more powerful hitters. They have a solid infield. The Flyers' coach is more experienced. He has coached many of the players for several years.

3. From this paragraph, you might conclude that

   A pitchers are the most important players on a baseball team

   B an experienced coach is better than powerful hitters

   C there are many things that make a good baseball team

   D young players are better than old players

4. How are the Flyers and Comets alike?

   F The teams play on the same field.

   G Both teams have great pitchers.

   H Both teams wear blue uniforms.

   J The teams have the same coach.

Juanita, Allie, and Sam were having a party.

"I don't know where to begin," said Sam.

"I'm not good at planning things either," said Allie.

"I've got some ideas," said Juanita. "Sam, you take care of the invitations. Allie, you plan the food. I'll take care of the music and the decorations."

"Good thinking," said Sam.

"I'll get started right away," agreed Allie.

5. What word describes Juanita?

   A lazy

   B organized

   C confused

   D forgetful

6. What can you conclude about Sam and Allie?

   F They are helpful but need direction.

   G They don't like Juanita's ideas.

   H They expect Juanita to do all the work.

   J They want to come to the party but are unwilling to help.

Contact lenses work like glasses. They help people see better. Contact lenses are small disks placed right on the eye. Glasses are worn on the face. Many people like contact lenses better than glasses. A group of people were asked how wearing contacts changed their lives. Some said they did better in sports. Others said they felt more attractive. Some people said that wearing contacts even helped them get better grades.

7. How are contacts lenses and glasses alike?

   A They help you make friends.

   B They help you see better.

   C They are small disks.

   D They are worn directly on the eyeball.

8. Choose the best summary of this passage.

   F Some contact lens wearers have become great athletes.

   G Contact lenses are better than glasses for everyone.

   H You see better with contacts because you wear them directly on your eye.

   J Some people say that wearing contacts has improved their vision and their lives.

Would you like to save water? Then don't take a bath. A quick shower will get you clean. Some people think showering is wasteful. They think that since the water hits your body once and runs down the drain, it is wasted. Bath water stays in the tub until you decide to let it out. The average tub holds about forty gallons of water. An eight-minute shower only uses about twenty gallons of water.

9. Choose the best paraphrase of this passage.

   A People should keep clean. They should take baths or showers.

   B Baths take longer than showers. A bathtub holds a lot of water.

   C When water runs down the drain, it is wasted. A shower wastes twenty gallons of water.

   D Some people think taking showers wastes water, but taking a shower uses less water than filling a bathtub.

10. What is the main idea of this passage?

   F Baths get you cleaner than showers.

   G Taking a shower is quicker than taking a bath.

   H Showering uses less water than taking a tub bath.

   J No one should waste water.

Extending Meaning

Connections

The ability to see how things and ideas fit together or connect is an important part of learning. What do you think the term *in common with* means?

_____

Think of connections you have in your life.
Name a person you have something in common with and explain what the connection is.

_____

_____

_____

_____

Do you think you have something in common with a person from a different culture or different country? Explain your answer.

_____

_____

_____

_____

_____

_____

_____

_____

Thought Association

What do you know about thought association? It refers to a way one word or idea suggests a related word or idea. For example, the word *airplane* can suggest the word *pilot* and the word *winter* can suggest the word *cold*. Write a related word for each of the words below.

morning _____   summer _____

baby _____   garden _____

travel _____   city _____

spicy _____   computer _____

job _____   friend _____

purple _____   lemon _____

lion _____   clock _____

Choose five pairs of words from above. Write a sentence using each pair of related words.

1. _____

_____

2. _____

_____

3. _____

_____

4. _____

_____

5. _____

_____

A ▶ Introduce

Predicting Outcomes

When you read, clues in the story can help you figure out what will happen next. This is called **predicting an outcome.**

> Lea and Jill both run the mile race. Lea has won the race for the last three years. However, she didn't train as hard this spring as she had in other years. Jill ran every day after school. Jill and Lea line up at the starting blocks.

1. What do you predict will happen next?

   A Jill will win the race.

   B Lea will win the race.

   C Jill will drop out of the race.

Yes, **(A)** Jill will probably win because she has been training.

Often you can predict what will happen by thinking about what has just happened.

> Miguel looked out the window. Dark clouds were gathering in the north. Soon the clouds covered the sun, and the wind began to blow. Just then Miguel remembered that he had left his book out on the patio.

2. What do you predict will happen next?

   A Miguel will play a video game with a friend.

   B Miguel will go out to the patio to get his book.

   C Miguel will go to the library to get another book.

Yes, **(B)** Miguel will go out to get his book before the storm.

> Kiya is an Alaskan sled dog. She has a coat of heavy fur that helps keep her warm. She likes to stand by the fireplace when she gets cold. Kiya was out in the snow all day long and got very cold.

3. What do you predict will happen next?

   A Kiya will pull a sled through the snow.

   B Kiya will sleep in the snow.

   C Kiya will stand by the fire.

Yes, **(C)** Kiya will stand by the fire because she is cold.

Circle the letter of the sentence that tells what is most likely to happen next.

Kate made sure her sister was not home. She got out the gift she had bought for her sister's birthday. Then she got out wrapping paper, tape, and ribbons.

1. **A** Kate takes the gift back to the store.

   B Kate gives her sister the gift.

   C Kate wraps the gift.

All day, Dale thought about his new computer. He had set up the computer last night. He was excited about learning how to use it. After school, he went right home.

2. **A** Dale goes out with his friends.

   B Dale watches television.

   C Dale turns on the computer.

Tonya's cat, Mittens, loves to eat tuna fish. Tonya began to make lunch. She opened a can of tuna fish and set it on the table. Just then the doorbell rang, and Tonya left the kitchen to answer the door.

3. **A** Mittens runs out the door when Tonya opens it.

   B Mittens takes a nap.

   C Mittens jumps onto the table and eats the tuna fish.

Tom smiled. How did his grandfather know he needed a new watch? It was the same watch that Tom had admired at the mall. Tom proudly wore his new watch every day. Saturday morning, he raked the yard. Later in the day, Tom noticed his watch was missing.

4. **A** Tom goes to the mall to look for a new watch.

   B Tom looks in the yard for his watch.

   C Tom tells his grandfather he doesn't like the watch.

C Apply

Read each paragraph. Circle the sentence that tells what probably happened next.

1. Max felt tired and thirsty after mowing the grass. He walked into the kitchen, got a glass, and went to the sink.

   Max washed the glass.

   Max poured himself a glass of milk.

   Max filled the glass with water.

2. Jana and Sue were supposed to meet at the movie theater at three o'clock. By three-thirty, Sue had not arrived. Jana took Sue's phone number out of her purse and got out a coin.

   Jana called Sue.

   Jana took the bus home.

   Jana bought a movie ticket for herself.

3. Bill hardly slept last night. He has spent weeks working on his science project—an electric car. The winner of the science fair would be posted on the school bulletin board this morning.

   Bill checked the bulletin board.

   Bill met his friends in the cafeteria.

   Bill went to shoot baskets in the gym.

4. Keith picked up the phone. Jim said, "The new music video you wanted to see is on right now!"

   Keith played a game.

   Keith turned on the television.

   Keith went for a walk.

5. Carmen met many new friends on her trip to Mexico. She knew she would not see them often. She wanted to remember what each of them looked like.

   Carmen wrote letters to her new friends.

   Carmen took pictures of her new friends.

   Carmen planned another trip.

◆D Check Up

Read each paragraph and circle the answer for each question.

Sam took a pan of muffins out of the oven. He said to his brother, "Have a muffin when they have cooled, Ben." As soon as Sam left the kitchen, Ben grabbed a muffin.

1. What probably happened next?

    A Sam made more muffins.

    B Ben burnt his fingers.

    C Ben washed the muffin pan.

    D Ben poured himself a glass of milk.

Meg and Patty had tickets to the soccer game. Meg was supposed to pick up Patty at ten o'clock. When she went outside, she saw her car had a flat tire.

2. What probably happened next?

    F Meg called Patty to say she would be late.

    G Meg decided to stay home.

    H Meg went to the soccer game without Patty.

    J Meg walked to the soccer game.

Tim enjoyed his woodworking class. He spent hours carving small wooden animals. His teacher said Tim was one of the best students he had. When the art festival came, Tim entered two of his best carvings.

3. What probably happened next?

    A Tim won a ribbon at the art festival.

    B Tim decided to learn to paint.

    C The judge didn't like Tim's carved animals.

    D Tim's teacher won a ribbon at the art festival.

Ana was watching television. Her brothers were talking in the same room. Ana could not hear the television very well.

4. What probably happened next?

    F Ana turned the television off.

    G Ana joined the conservation.

    H Ana turned the lights off in the room.

    J Ana turned the volume on the television louder.

A Introduce

Predicting Outcomes

You can use what you have read and what you already know to predict what will happen next in a story.

> Dolores has been campaigning for weeks. She wants to be the new mayor. She has talked with people and has good ideas for improving services and reducing taxes. Her opponent Ed hasn't campaigned at all. Tomorrow is election day.

What do I know from the story?

Story Clues:

Dolores has been campaigning for weeks. She has talked with people and has good ideas for improving services and reducing taxes.

What do I know from previous experience?

Experience Clues:

People vote for hard-working, knowledgeable candidates.

Prediction:

_____

> Barb backed her car into the parking spot. She didn't hear the sound of glass crunching under the tires. When she came out of the store, she saw that the car was tilted at a strange angle.

Use clues from the story and what you already know to predict what might happen next.

Story Clues:

_____

Experience Clues:

_____

Prediction:

_____

B Practice

Use clues from the story and what you already know to make predictions. Circle the sentence that best predicts the outcome.

1. Paulo worked hard to improve his math grade. He turned in all of his homework on time, studied for every test, and even did some extra work. His teacher, Ms. Cook said, "Paulo, I'm so proud of you. I couldn't have done better myself!"

   Mrs. Cook was disappointed in Paulo.

   Paulo got a poor grade in math.

   Paulo got an A in math.

2. "Jesse," said Jack, "do you really think we will be able to ride 25 miles? It seems like an awfully long distance on a bike."
   "Quit worrying," said Jesse, "Have I ever signed up for a bike ride we couldn't finish? Let's get going."

   Jack and Jesse started riding their bikes.

   Jack went home.

   Jesse went home.

3. Tina looked out the hotel window. The streets of New York were very different from the streets of the small town where she lived. She wanted to explore the city.

   Tina went for a walk along the busy streets of New York.

   Tina wrote postcards to her friends telling them about New York.

   Tina read a book about living in New York City.

4. Bob needed a new car. Without carefully shopping, he bought one. The car's body was covered with dents and much of the paint was scraped off. When Bob started the engine, it made a coughing noise and the car began to shake.

   Bob realized that this is best purchase he ever made.

   Bob decided to buy new tires for his car.

   Bob realized that the car will probably break down in a short while.

Use clues from the story and what you already know to predict what might happen next.

Hannah filled out the job application carefully. She wrote down all her previous experience and filled in the names of two employers who would speak well of her. She dressed neatly for the interview and spoke clearly and politely.

1. What do you think the outcome will be?

_____

Dave measured the flour, salt, yeast, and water. He kneaded the dough and put it into a bread pan. He put the pan in the oven but forgot to set the timer. Later he saw smoke coming from the kitchen.

2. What do you think the outcome will be?

_____

Mr. Lee was traveling to a small town. He studied a road map before he left. However, he didn't know that the town had a big snowfall the day before. When Mr. Lee got to the town, the signs were covered with snow.

3. What do you think the outcome will be?

_____

Jane had a new camera. All of her friends had come over and Jane didn't take time to read the instruction booklet. Jane took pictures and sent the film to a photo shop. The owner of the photo shop called.

4. What do you think the outcome will be?

_____

D ▸ Check Up

Read each paragraph and circle the answer for each question.

Lynne was taking a three-week trip to the east coast. She had asked a neighbor to water her plants while she was away. As Lynne boarded the plane to come home, she felt her house keys in the bottom of her purse. She had forgotten to give her neighbor her keys.

1. What do you think the outcome will be?

   A Lynne's plants are healthy when she returns.

   B Lynne decides to drive home instead of fly.

   C Lynne's plants are wilted from lack of water.

   D Lynne cannot get into her house when she returns.

Terry was training her dog to roll over. She knew that it liked dog treats. First Terry made the dog roll over when she said, "Roll over." Then she gave it a treat. Terry did this several times each day.

2. What do you think the outcome will be?

   F The dog sits up when he sees a dog treat.

   G Her dog learns to roll over.

   H Terry finds out that you can't teach her dog tricks.

   J The dog barks when it wants to go outside.

The Wonder Dogs were the city's most popular rock band. Tickets for their concert went on sale at nine o'clock Saturday morning. Chang decided to sleep in when his alarm went off at eight-thirty. He got to the ticket office at noon.

3. What do you think the outcome will be?

   A Chang gets great seats for the concert.

   B Chang's concert tickets come in the mail that day.

   C Chang does not get tickets to the concert.

   D The Wonder Dogs cancel the concert.

 **Read On** Read "Electric Cars." Answer the questions and make predictions about what you have read.

 **Introduce**

Identifying Fact and Opinion

When you read, you need to be able to separate facts from opinions. Facts can be proved. Opinions tell what people believe or think. Sometimes sentences have words that can help you identify them as opinions. These words include *believe, think, best, all,* and *everyone.*

A fact is a statement that can be proved.
Carrots, beets, and potatoes are vegetables.

An opinion is a person's idea or belief.
Jon thinks potatoes are the tastiest vegetables.

Read each pair of sentences. Circle the sentence that is a fact.

1. Red and yellow are colors.

   Red is a prettier color than yellow.

2. Dogs and cats are mammals.

   Dogs make better pets than cats.

3. It would be fun to hunt for fossils.

   Fossils can be found on Earth.

4. Vincent van Gogh painted the still-life "Sunflowers."

   Van Gogh was the best artist of the nineteenth century.

5. The roller coaster is the most exciting ride at the park.

   Tivoli Gardens is one of the world's oldest amusement parks.

6. Factories that pollute water supplies should be fined.

   Sewage and chemicals from factories cause water pollution.

7. No one should travel without a map.

   Maps show distance and direction.

8. All citizens of the United States have rights.

   Children should have the same rights as adults.

B Practice

Read each sentence. Ask yourself if the sentence states something that can be proved. Circle either *fact* or *opinion*.

1. Jim reads the morning newspaper on the train.

   fact   opinion

2. The guitar, violin, and harp are stringed instruments.

   fact   opinion

3. Earth's path around the sun is nearly 600 million miles long.

   fact   opinion

4. I think that someday people will live in space.

   fact   opinion

5. I believe that Lou Gehrig was the greatest baseball player of all time.

   fact   opinion

6. Light is a form of energy that travels in rays.

   fact   opinion

7. I like visiting the National Air and Space Museum.

   fact   opinion

8. Wayne Gretzky is the highest scorer in the National Hockey League's history.

   fact   opinion

9. New York City is the headquarters for the United Nations.

   fact   opinion

10. Eleanor Roosevelt was the most influential First Lady.

    fact   opinion

11. General Colin Powell was the first African American to head the
    U.S. military forces.

    fact   opinion

C Apply

Read the sentence. Write *F* on the line if the sentence states a fact. Write *O* if the sentence states an opinion.

_____ 1. Many communities have shelters for abandoned animals.

_____ 2. Some animals live in animal shelters.

_____ 3. A veterinarian gives medical care to sick animals.

_____ 4. People should be more responsible pet owners.

_____ 5. Many pets are abandoned during the summer.

_____ 6. It is not fun to travel with a big dog in the car.

_____ 7. This animal shelter was founded twenty years ago.

_____ 8. Anyone with free time should volunteer there.

_____ 9. Anyone who adopts a cat or dog gets a month's supply of food.

_____10. The vet, Dr. Wilson, is the kindest man in town.

D Check Up

Circle the answer for each question.

1. Which sentence states an opinion?

   A A tiger can be seven feet long and weigh 500 pounds.

   B Tigers are the most beautiful animals.

   C A tiger's stripes help it hide in its surroundings.

   D Tigers live in grasslands and forests.

2. Which sentence states a fact?

   F I believe in recycling paper, glass, and aluminum.

   G All communities should require recycling.

   H The largest amount of American trash is packaging.

   J I don't like to use plastic containers.

3. Which sentence states a fact?

   A In the Old West, many people lived on small ranches.

   B Ranching was more difficult than farming.

   C Every rancher became very wealthy.

   D I think the work would be too hard.

4. Which sentence states a opinion?

   F Rice is a basic food for nearly half the world's people.

   G Rice is tastier than potatoes.

   H Rice farming is important in many Asian countries.

   J Rice is a grain.

5. Which sentence states a fact?

   A I think an ostrich is a funny-looking bird.

   B In South Africa, the ostrich is ridden in races, like a horse.

   C I believe it takes a special kind of jockey to ride an ostrich.

   D I wouldn't like to ride a three-hundred pound bird with a nasty temper.

6. Which sentence states an opinion?

   F There are 54 national parks in the United States.

   G The world's first national park was Yellowstone.

   H We should be very proud of our national park system.

   J Millions of people visit the parks each year.

Identifying Fact and Opinion

One way to identify a sentence that states an opinion is to look for clue words such as *believe, think, like, dislike, all, best,* and *everyone.*

Opinion　　I think apples are better tasting than oranges.
Opinion　　I like watermelon better than grapefruit.

If these words are not used, think about whether the sentence tells a person's idea, belief, or judgment.

Fact　　　　Basketball was invented in 1891 by James Naismith.
Opinion　　Basketball is more difficult to play than baseball.

Read each pair of sentences. If the sentence states a fact, write *F* on the line. If the sentence states an opinion, write *O* on the line.

1. _____ A box turtle can live to be 100 years old.

   _____ Twenty-five is the best age to be.

2. _____ The pyramids of Egypt were built as royal tombs.

   _____ Egypt is a fascinating place to visit.

3. _____ Everyone should use a calculator to check his or her homework.

   _____ In ancient times, people used an abacus for computing.

4. _____ People who carpool should get gas at discount prices.

   _____ The cost of gas varies from place to place.

5. _____ Crocodiles are large reptiles.

   _____ A hot climate is better than a cold one.

Read each sentence and decide whether it is a fact or opinion. If the sentence states a fact, write *Fact* on the line. If the sentence states an opinion, write *Opinion* on the line and underline the clue word.

1. _____ Grebes are birds that can dive.

2. _____ I think the grebe is the bird kingdom's swimming champ.

3. _____ Grebes can swim at birth.

4. _____ Grebes build grass nests that float on water.

5. _____ When grebe chicks get tired during a swim, they rest in air pockets under their mother's wings.

6. _____ This must make the chicks feel safe.

7. _____ When courting a mate, grebes do complicated underwater dances.

8. _____ Dancing underwater cannot be easy.

9. _____ Grebes look like ducks with large heads.

10. _____ Their head feathers look like crowns to me.

11. _____ Grebes have almost no tail.

12. _____ Their feet are not webbed.

13. _____ They are the world's most awkward birds.

14. _____ Grebes often have difficulty taking off.

15. _____ They can fly long distances.

C Apply

Read the sentence. Write *F* on the line if the sentence states a fact. Write *O* if the sentence states an opinion.

1. _____ In Spanish, *Nevada* means "snow covered."

2. _____ Rhode Island is the smallest state.

3. _____ California has the most beautiful scenery.

4. _____ Virginia was the birthplace of eight presidents.

5. _____ The friendliest people live in Minnesota.

6. _____ *Ohio* is the Iroquois word for "good river."

7. _____ The people of Alaska wear the warmest clothes.

8. _____ Hawaii is made up entirely of islands.

9. _____ Michigan is a good place to ski.

10. _____ Oregon produces more timber than any other state.

11. _____ The weather is always great in Utah.

12. _____ Vermont is famous for granite and maple syrup.

13. _____ Delaware was the first state of the United States.

14. _____ I like the wide open spaces of Wyoming.

15. _____ The first free public library was in New Hampshire.

D ▷ Check Up

Circle the answer for each question.

1. Which sentence states a fact?

   A My little brother is too noisy.

   B My sister has the coolest car in the neighborhood.

   C My mother is a dentist.

   D My dad is a great cook.

2. Which sentence states an opinion?

   F Saturn's rings are made of chunks of ice.

   G Jupiter is the most fascinating planet.

   H Mercury is covered with craters.

   J Earth is 93 million miles from the sun.

3. Which sentence states a fact?

   A Thomas Edison invented the phonograph.

   B The zipper is the most useful invention.

   C I think everyone should have a computer.

   D Life would be boring without television.

4. Which sentence states an opinion?

   F United States coins are made of a mixture of metals.

   G Pennies should be taken out of circulation.

   H The Bureau of Engraving designs and prints all paper money.

   J Portraits of presidents appear on some American coins.

5. Which sentence states an opinion?

   A Halley's Comet can be seen every 76 years.

   B The galaxy we live in is called the Milky Way.

   C The Big Dipper points in the direction of the North Star.

   D It is good luck to see a shooting star.

6. Which sentence states an opinion?

   F The largest city in the United States is New York, New York.

   G The city with the best weather is Denver, Colorado.

   H The oldest city in the United States is St. Augustine, Florida.

   J The southernmost city in the United Sates is Hilo, Hawaii.

Read On   Read "Pride of the Giants." Answer the questions and look for facts and opinions in the article.

Applying Passage Elements

When you read, you often use elements in the passage to extend meaning. You can make a judgment or draw a conclusion based on the facts you have read.

Read the paragraph. Then use what you have read to extend the meaning.

A coat of arms is a shield with designs that represents a family. The designs or symbols usually stand for important events in the history of the family. Coats of arms began with knights of the Middle Ages. Knights fought in armor. On the battlefield, one knight looked much like another. So knights began sewing symbols on the coats they wore over their armor. Each knight had his own symbol.

1. Wearing a coat of arms helped a knight

   A keep his armor clean

   B tell a friend from an enemy

   C keep warm in cold weather

On the battlefield friends and enemies looked alike. Wearing a coat of arms helped a knight **(B)** tell a friend from an enemy

Read the paragraph. Then use what you have read to extend the meaning.

Greenland isn't green. If fact, it's even icier than Iceland. Greenland's name was intended to confuse people. In A.D. 982, Eric the Red, a Norse explorer, discovered this island. It was bitter cold and covered with ice and snow. But he wanted people to move there to start a colony. So he named it Greenland. Soon after, twenty-five ships full of settlers sailed for the icy land.

2. Eric the Red thought people would not move to Greenland because

   A of the bitter climate

   B they didn't like to fish

   C it was far from home

Use elements from the passage to answer each question.

The Maoris of New Zealand use their hands to catch fish. The fish often hide near rocks. The Maoris walk into the water very quietly and sneak up behind the fish. The fishers reach down to gently tickle the fish. When the fish tries to get away, it is trapped by the rock. The fishers then scoop up the fish with their hands.

1. Which of following statements about the Maoris is false?

   A Fish are not a part of the Maoris diet.

   B The Maoris fish without poles or nets.

   C The Maoris fish without hooks or bait.

Color-blind people have trouble telling certain colors apart. For some, red and green look the same. Others confuse blue and yellow. In rare cases, color-blind people can't see colors at all. They see everything in shades of black, white, and gray.

2. Which of the following would **not** be helpful to a person who is color-blind?

   A the shape of a traffic sign

   B the size of a traffic sign

   C the color of lights on a traffic light

Some animals have special features that help protect them from their enemies. The coats of some animals change seasonally to match the color of their surroundings.

3. What color does the coat of an Arctic fox turn in winter?

   A brown

   B black

   C white

The old expression "A stitch in time saves nine" means that taking the time to make a small repair may eliminate the need for major repairs later. A related expression is "An ounce of prevention is worth a pound of cure."

4. Which person below is putting the expression to practical use?

   A Nan completes her project two days before it is due.

   B Jorge goes to see his doctor every year for a checkup.

   C Todd treats others as he would like to be treated.

C Apply

Read each paragraph. Put a check mark next to the sentence that tells what you have learned from each paragraph.

In 1891, James Naismith invented the game of basketball as an indoor sport to be played between football and baseball seasons. The object of the game was to toss a soccer ball into a peach basket nailed to the wall. Because there were eighteen players when the game was invented, there were nine players on each team. Later, the five-player rule was adopted. Today basketball is played outdoors and indoors all over the world.

1. _____ Basketball is more popular than baseball or football.

   _____ Basketball has changed over the years.

   _____ Basketball can be played by any number of people.

What time of day were you born? Some scientists think that the time at which a person is born affects the way that person feels every day. People have an internal clock that helps run their bodies. Some people feel tired in the morning and perky in the evening. Some scientists think that people's internal clocks are set at the time they are born. They think people born in the morning prefer mornings. People born at night prefer evenings.

2. _____ People who are born in the morning are full of energy at night.

   _____ People who are born in the morning tend to be early birds.

   _____ People who are born in the morning like to stay up late at night.

Like whales and porpoises, dolphins are mammals, not fish. Dolphins feed their young with mother's milk, have lungs, and are warm-blooded. Dolphins breathe through a blowhole, a nostril on the top of their heads.

3. _____ Dolphins can stay underwater all the time.

   _____ Dolphins breathe through gills.

   _____ Dolphins come to the surface to breathe.

Circle the answer for each question.

An old custom says that the way a baby holds a coin shows how the baby will use money when he or she grows up. If the baby holds the coin tightly, the child will be a person who saves money. If the child holds the coin loosely, people say the child will be generous.

1. According to this custom, a child who drops a coin

   A will grow up to be rich

   B will grow up to find money laying on the ground

   C will grow up to be careless about money

   D will grow up to be a banker

Why does an ice cube float? You might expect ice to sink in water. It floats because it is less dense than water. The water molecules in ice have more space between them than the molecules in liquid water have.

2. Which of the following sentences is true?

   F Ice evaporates quicker than water.

   G A cup of ice has fewer molecules than a cup of water.

   H Ice cubes melt quickly in cold water.

   J A cup of ice has more molecules than a cup of water.

Venice is an Italian city built upon 120 islands in the Adriatic Sea. More than 150 canals take the place of streets on all the islands of Venice.

3. The chief form of transportation in Venice is

   A cars

   B boats

   C airplanes

   D trains

Eyes don't lie. You pretend to be nice to someone you don't like, but people looking in your eyes may be able to tell how you really feel. Pupils grow larger when you look at someone you are fond of. If you look at someone you don't like, your pupils will become smaller.

4. Which of the following sentences is true?

   F Your pupils will change size depending on how you feel about the person you are looking at.

   G Pupils change size depending on your eye color.

   H The size of your pupils always remains the same.

   J The pupils of honest people are larger than those of dishonest people.

A Introduce

Applying Passage Elements

Sometimes you can apply passage elements as well as things you already know to extend the meaning of what you read.

Read each paragraph and use passage elements to answer the questions.

As Angie sped across the frozen lake, she looked at the hills that surrounded her. The trees were bare, except for the icicles that hung from their branches. She had completed an exact figure eight when she saw her friends approach. Angie leaped as high as she could, spun twice in the air, and landed perfectly on the edge of her blade.

1. The story takes place in

   A summer

   B fall

   C winter

   The frozen lake, the icicles, and *the bare trees* show that the story takes place in **(C)** winter.

2. Which phrase best describes Angie?

   A a beginner skater

   B a very good skater

   C a frightened skater

   Exact figure eight, leaped as high as she could, spun twice in the air, and *landed perfectly* show that Angie is **(B)** a very good skater.

Rick took a quick look down the street before he entered the concert hall. If any of his friends found out he was here, he would never hear the end of it. Suddenly the curtain rose and the music filled the hall. For the next several hours, Rick watched the singers act as the story unfolded. Rick enjoyed the operatic voices. At the end, he clapped for an encore. As the curtain fell, Rick put on his coat and slipped out the back door.

3. What is Rick doing?

   A watching a movie

   B watching a ballet

   C watching an opera

4. Why does Rick slip out the back door?

   A He does not want to run into any of his friends.

   B His seat is closer to the back door.

   C He is in a hurry to get home.

◆B▶ Practice

Read each paragraph and underline the phrase that best completes each sentence.

If you burn your skin, you can speed the healing and lessen the pain with correct first aid. First, run cold water over the burn to stop the burning process. If the burn looks white or tan instead of pink, feels numb, or is larger than a two-inch square, seek medical help. Don't apply aloe vera, butter, or any ointment to the burn. Any covering on the burn will block healing oxygen.

1. When you've burned your skin,

   A you should apply first-aid cream

   B its important to keep it protected from air

   C touching it with anything but cold water can do more harm than good

The kangaroo rat has strong hind legs like a kangaroo. However, it is only four or five inches long. Its strong hind legs help it run from enemies. It can also hear an enemy from far way.

2. The kangaroo rat

   A can attack animals larger than itself

   B protects itself without being a fighter

   C is very similar to a kangaroo

Some people believe than an omen is a sign that predicts the future. The Duke of Buckingham believed in omens. One day he found that his picture had fallen out of its frame. From that day on, he waited for disaster to happen. He lived without a moment's peace. Because of a piece of frayed string, or perhaps a strong gust of wind, he lived his life in fear.

3. Omens are much like

   A practical jokes

   B truths

   C superstitions

Read each paragraph. Put a check mark next to the sentence that tells what you can determine by using passage elements to extend meaning.

For hundreds of years, English sailors got a disease called scurvy. Then a doctor found that people who ate citrus fruits did not get scurvy. So beginning in 1800, every English ship carried lime juice. Each day the sailors drank the juice. Soon the sailors stopped getting scurvy. Scurvy is caused by a lack of vitamin C. Before they began drinking lime juice, sailors had only dried meat, bread, and cheese to eat.

1. _____ Scurvy is caused by eating too much dried meat and cheese.

   _____ Citrus fruits are a good source of vitamin C.

   _____ English sailors have always been healthy.

When people think of the American West, they usually think of horses. But Native Americans did not even know what a horse looked like until the 1500s. At that time, the Spanish brought horses to North America. They set up towns and missions. They gave or sold horses to the Native Americans. Travelers in the 1700s could cross the continent without seeing a single wild horse.

2. _____ Native Americans always rode horses.

   _____ Horses were not found in North America before the 1500s.

   _____ The Spanish were better riders than the Native Americans.

The most expensive wool is the world is cashmere. Cashmere comes from goats. These goats live is the part of India known as Kashmir. Kashmir is high in the Himalaya Mountains. People have tried to raise the goats in other parts of the world, with no success.

3. _____ Cashmere is grown on plants.

   _____ Cashmere comes from sheep raised in the United States.

   _____ Cashmere is costly because it is rare and hard to obtain.

Circle the answer for each question.

In Iceland there are Roman coins from the third century. Iceland is thousands of miles from Rome. Experts don't think the Romans sailed that far north. They don't think the Romans knew about Iceland. There is no mention of Iceland in Roman writings.

1. How the coins got to Iceland is a
   A fact
   B legend
   C mystery
   D joke

Few people trying to "make ends meet" know where the phrase comes from. Long ago, sailing ships had hundreds of ropes that held the masts and sails in place. If one of those ropes broke, sailors had to replace or repair it. The ship owners didn't want to spend the money for more rope. They told the sailors to tie the broken rope together. This meant stretching the rope to make both ends meet.

2. In everyday speech "making ends meet" means
   F not fixing anything
   G stretching the money you have
   H using rope to tie your belongings together
   J fixing everything

Sea otters are animals that live in groups near the coast of Alaska. Otters sleep in patches of seaweed. People hunted otters for their fur. New laws now protect them.

3. Because of new laws
   A people are making pets of otters
   B the cost of otter fur is decreasing
   C the otter population is growing
   D otters are living on land

Ants live in colonies and work hard. Although they are smart, it is easy for an ant to get lost. Ants follow trails that other ants have made. But if the trail runs in a circle, ants don't know enough to leave it. They often walk around the circle until they fall dead.

4. If ants were smarter, they would make a new
   F colony
   G circle
   H trail
   J anthill

Read On   Read "Life Beneath a Blanket of Snow." Answer the questions and apply passage elements to extend meaning.

Predicting Outcomes

You can use clues in the story to figure out what will happen next. This is called predicting an outcome.

Will was giving a speech at work. He was not looking forward to giving the speech. "What if I forget my speech?" he asked his co-worker. "You have practiced your speech for weeks," said Lisa. "You'll be great." Will admitted to himself that he was well prepared. Suddenly it was his turn to speak. He took a deep breath.

Prediction: Will should make a good speech because he has practiced.

Identifying Fact and Opinion

A fact is something that can be proved.

An opinion is someone's idea or belief. An opinion cannot be proved.

Calypso music comes from Trinidad. (fact)
I think an expert calypso singer uses clever words. (opinion)

Applying Passage Elements

You can use elements in the passage to extend meaning.

Some people call the standby players on a football team the taxi squad. At one time, the owner of a team had money problems. He couldn't afford to pay all his players. He offered them another job. He also owned a taxi company.

Extend the meaning: Because the owner had a taxi company, he most likely made his players taxi drivers.

Assessment

Read the paragraphs and circle the answer for each question.

I think Earth was misnamed. The word *earth* means land. Our planet's surface is more than 70 percent water. Earth is unique among the planets. It is the only one to have oceans. It has four oceans; the Pacific, the Atlantic, the Indian, and the Arctic.

1. Which sentence states an opinion?

   A I think Earth was misnamed.

   B The word *earth* means land.

   C Earth is unique among the planets.

   D It is the only one to have oceans.

2. It seems that Earth was

   F named by people who lived near an ocean

   G once was 70 percent land

   H named for the part of the planet people are most familiar with

   J once covered by mountains

Sean looked out into the yard after the snowstorm. An animal had left tracks. The tracks looked like hooves with dots behind them. He decided to play a joke on his sister. He put on one boot. He hopped around the yard. His sister would be home in three hours. Meanwhile it started to snow again.

3. The tracks Sean saw in the snow were probably made by

   A a car

   B an elephant

   C a sled

   D a deer

4. What do you predict will happen?

   F His sister will make tracks in the snow.

   G The snow will cover the tracks Sean made.

   H His sister will see a one-legged animal making tracks.

   J The snow will melt before Sean's sister gets home.

Most people think that all lions look alike. However, you can tell lions apart by their whiskers. Lions' whiskers grow in tufts. The holes that their whiskers grow out of are arranged in groups. I think only an animal trainer can safely get close enough to see the differences.

5. Which statement is not a fact?

   A You can tell lions apart by their whiskers.

   B Lions' whiskers grow in tufts.

   C The holes that their whiskers grow out of are arranged in groups.

   D I think only an animal trainer can safely get close enough to see the differences.

6. Based on what you read in the passage, which statement is true?

   F On each lion, the groups of whiskers are arranged in a different pattern.

   G You can tell lions apart by the color of their whiskers.

   H There is no way to tell lions apart.

   J All lions look exactly alike.

Her mom thinks Nicki is forgetful. One morning, Nicki went to the barn to milk the cows. After she finished, she placed the pail of milk in front of the barn door. As she walked out of the barn, she turned to call to her mom.

7. What do you think probably happened?

   A Nicki forgot to milk the cows.

   B Nicki tripped over the pail of milk.

   C Nicki's mom milked the cows.

   D Nicki drank the milk from the pail.

8. Which sentence is an opinion?

   F Her mom thinks Nicki is forgetful.

   G One morning, Nicki went to the barn to milk the cows.

   H After she finished, she placed the pail of milk in front of the barn door.

   J As she walked out of the barn, she turned to call to her mom.

A full moon in fall is called a harvest moon. This name comes from a time when farmers had to harvest their crops by hand. They worked from dawn to as long as they had light to harvest their crops. With the large full moon, they had enough light to continue harvesting. They had to get their crops in before winter.

9. Why is the harvest moon no longer as important to farmers?

   A Farmers don't work as long into the night.

   B Farmers use modern machinery to harvest their crops.

   C Farmers don't harvest their crops before winter.

   D Farmers like to harvest in the dark.

Pat believes that the cost of gas is higher than necessary. The price of gas has increased more than a dollar a gallon since last year. At this rate Pat will spend over $1,000 more this year for gas than he did last year. He has written to his state representative. He has limited his driving. Pat thinks the cost of gas will come down early next year.

10. What action would probably reduce Pat's gas cost?

   F protesting in front of the gas station

   G arranging a carpool with a fellow worker

   H purchasing gas in a state where the cost of gas is less

   J campaigning for a candidate who promises to lower fuel taxes

Posttest

Circle the word that is spelled correctly and best completes each sentence.

1. _____ are my car keys?

   A Where

   B Wear

   C Were

   D Ware

2. She _____ the bags out to the car.

   F carryed

   G carried

   H caried

   J carryied

3. The teens are _____ on the frozen pond.

   A skateng

   B skatting

   C skateing

   D skating

4. Will the dog _____ the stick?

   F reitrieve

   G retreive

   H retrieve

   J retriev

Read the graph and circle the answer for each question.

Favorite Radio Stations

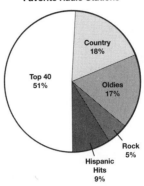

5. What percentage of people listen to rock music?

   A 18%

   B 17%

   C 5%

   D 9%

6. What kind of music do most people listen to?

   F Country

   G Hispanic Hits

   H Top 40

   J Oldies

7. How many more people listen to Country than to Oldies?

   A 1%

   B 17%

   C 18%

   D 10%

8. What kind of music do the least number of people listen to?

   F Rock

   G Hispanic Hits

   H Top 40

   J Oldies

Circle the answer that tells what the symbol means.

9.

A merge
B walk
C yield
D stop

10.

F exit
G hospital
H school
J restaurant

11.

A no U-turn
B no right turn
C divided highway
D no left turn

12.

F bus stop
G telephone
H camping
J baggage airport

13.

A poison
B recycle
C no smoking
D exit

14.

F no bicycles
G walk
H signal ahead
J don't walk

Read the map and circle the answer for each question.

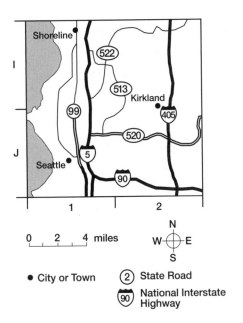

Shoreline

522

513
Kirkland

99

405

520

5

Seattle

90

1   2

0   2   4 miles

N
W ⊕ E
S

• City or Town

② State Road

90 National Interstate Highway

15. What kind of road is route 5?

  A interstate highway

  B state highway

  C unpaved road

  D county highway

16. What are the coordinates for Seattle?

  F H2

  G G1

  H J1

  J K3

17. About how far is it from Seattle to Shoreline?

  A 100 miles

  B 9 miles

  C 3 miles

  D 50 miles

Read the paragraphs and circle the answer for each question.

When Len arrived at the grocery store, it was filled with shoppers. "Oh, no," Len said to himself as he saw the checkout line. "There are four people ahead of me and each one has a full cart of groceries. I'm going to be here for at least a half hour."

Just then the store manager approached him. "Good morning, sir," he said with a smile. "I see you have a small order. Follow me to the express line. I'll have you out of here in a flash."

18. How would you describe the store manager?

  F rude

  G lazy

  H helpful

  J angry

19. The express line is for customers who

  A have small orders

  B talk to the manager

  C are impatient

  D deserve better service

20. How many people were in line ahead of Len?

  F half a dozen

  G four

  H none

  J one

All animals need food to survive. The penguin has layers of fat that allow it to fast for an entire month. The fat keeps it warm. It also supplies the penguin's body with food. Most people need to eat daily. Some people eat three meals day. Others eat more or less frequently. Some people like to eat small amounts throughout the day. Others think it is healthier to eat a large portion once or twice a day.

21. In the sentence "The penguin has layers of fat that allow it to fast for an entire month," what does *fast* mean?

A eat way too much

B move quickly

C go without food

D think quickly

22. What is the main idea of this paragraph?

F People and animals have the same eating patterns.

G Animals and people store and use food differently.

H Fasting is unhealthy.

J People have more healthy diets than penguins.

23. Which sentence states an opinion?

A All animals need food to survive.

B Some people eat three meals day.

C Others eat more or less frequently.

D Others think it is healthier to eat once or twice a day.

Do you sing in the shower? Most people have only a few places where they will sing. It's surprising, but birds are the same way. They don't sing all the time. Like people, birds only sing in certain places. They prefer to sing perched in trees or when they are flying. They don't normally sing when on the ground.

24. According the paragraph how are people and birds alike?

    F They take showers.

    G They sing when they are surprised.

    H They sing only in certain places.

    J They sing only when they are on the ground.

25. What is a synonym for *prefer?*

    A pretend

    B like

    C hope

    D decide

26. Why don't birds sing all the time?

    F not stated

    G They only sing when people are around to hear them.

    H They can't sing and fly at the same time.

    J Singing attracts enemies.

When you're relaxed, your heart beats sixty to eighty times per minute. When you're running or dancing, your heart rate may double. That is because your muscles use more oxygen when you're active. More blood is needed to carry the oxygen. So your heart beats faster. All animals have different heart rates. The smaller the animal, the faster the heart rate. For example, a hummingbird's heart beats one thousand times per minute. An ostrich's heart beats sixty to seventy times per minute.

27. Why does your heart beat faster when you're active?

   A You feel better when your heart rate doubles.

   B More blood is needed to carry oxygen to your muscles.

   C Your muscles need to relax.

   D An increased heart rate makes you run faster.

28. From this paragraph, you can conclude that

   F all birds have the same heart rate

   G animals have different heart rates, depending on their size

   H exercise is unhealthy because it doubles your heart rate

   J all animals have the same heart rate

29. Using what you have learned in the paragraph, what do you predict a 20-foot whale's heart rate is?

   A two thousand times per minute

   B sixty times per minute

   C nine times per minute

   D one hundred times per minute

Proper first aid can save a victim's life. It can also prevent more medical problems. First analyze the situation. Decide whether you can help the victim. If you are unsure, do not attempt treatment. Follow these general steps when giving first aid. Call for help. Then provide urgent care. If the victim is bleeding severely or has stopped breathing, treatment must begin at once. Next examine the person for other injuries. Finally, if needed, treat the victim for shock.

30. Which of the following would you **not** call for emergency medical service?

   F fire department

   G police

   H your family physician

   J hospital

31. After you have called for help, what is the next step in giving first aid?

   A Treat the victim for shock.

   B Examine the victim for additional injuries.

   C Fill out an accident report.

   D Provide urgent care.

32. What is an antonym for *prevent?*

   F cause

   G prescribe

   H stop

   J increase

Posttest Answer Key and Evaluation Chart

This posttest has been designed to check your mastery of the reading skills studied. Circle the question numbers that you answered incorrectly and review the practice pages covering those skills. Carefully rework those practice pages to be sure you understand those skills.

Key

1.	A
2.	G
3.	D
4.	H
5.	C
6.	H
7.	A
8.	F
9.	D
10.	G
11.	A
12.	G
13.	B
14.	J
15.	A
16.	H
17.	B
18.	H
19.	A
20.	G
21.	C
22.	G
23.	D
24.	H
25.	B
26.	F
27.	B
28.	G
29.	C
30.	H
31.	D
32.	F

Tested Skills	Question Numbers	Practice Pages
Synonyms	25	21–24, 25–28
Antonyms	32	29–32, 33–36
Context clues	21	37–40, 41–44
Spelling	1, 2, 3, 4	45–48, 49–52
Details	20	59–62, 63–66
Sequence	31	67–70, 71–74
Stated concepts	26	75–78, 79–82
Signs	9, 10, 11, 12, 13, 14	89–92
Maps	15, 16, 17	93–96
Graphs	5, 6, 7, 8	97–100, 101–104
Characters	18	119–122, 123–126
Main idea	22	127–130, 131–134
Compare/contrast	24	135–138, 139–142
Drawing conclusions	19, 28	143–146, 147–150, 151–154
Cause and effect	27	155–158, 159–162, 163–166
Predicting outcomes	29	181–184, 185–188
Identifying fact and opinion	23	189–192, 193–196
Applying passage elements	30	197–200, 201–204

◆ Answer Key

◆ Unit 1 Words in Context

Page 19: Baseball: fly, home run, out, outfield; Bowling: spare, split, gutter, frame; Football: down, punt, huddle, hike; Basketball: slam dunk, dribble, traveling, jump ball
Answers will vary.

Page 20: 1. crowded around, **2.** older person who supervises younger people, **3.** completely soaked, **4.** brought back, **5.** combined

◆ Lesson 1 Recognizing Synonyms

Page 21: 1. calm, **2.** intelligent, **3.** humorous, **4.** leap, **5.** sick, **6.** automobile, **7.** stroll, **8.** pail, **9.** talk, **10.** halt
Possible answers: **11.** beautiful, **12.** unusual, **13.** things, **14.** fast, **15.** asked, **16.** bag, **17.** unhappy, **18.** fragrance, **19.** road, **20.** store

Page 22: 1. A, **2.** H, **3.** C, **4.** G, **5.** D, **6.** H, **7.** B, **8.** J, **9.** D, **10.** F

Page 23: Possible answers: **1.** The weather was very pleasant for April. **2.** She spoke softly to the child. **3.** The toddler clutched her teddy bear. **4.** That vase is suitable for those flowers. **5.** Climbing up the mountain was difficult. **6.** Your parent loves you unconditionally. **7.** She heard weird noises coming from the basement. **8.** They built a summer home in the mountains. **9.** We had an enjoyable evening at the concert. **10.** Tom was disappointed that he missed your visit.

Page 24: 1. normally, **2.** famous, **3.** rushed, **4.** address, **5.** filthy, **6.** crowd, **7.** aroma, **8.** noisily, **9.** composed

◆ Lesson 2 Using Synonyms

Page 25: 1. seat, **2.** blossom, **3.** tale, **4.** awkward, **5.** strange, **6.** teach, **7.** correct, **8.** sadness, **9.** picture, **10.** easily

Page 26: 1. I put the old clothes in a sturdy carton. **2.** He would like to relax for an hour after work. **3.** The basement was untidy after band practice. **4.** These two stories are similar. **5.** The explorers are trying to locate the sunken ship. **6.** The church gave help to the storm victims. **7.** The circus act will thrill the children. **8.** A chilly wind blew off the ocean. **9.** I always feel sleepy after lunch.

Page 27: Possible answers: **1.** The squirrel scurried away quickly. **2.** She gave the inexpensive things to her dog. **3.** He is in a big rush every morning. **4.** There are deep potholes in the road. **5.** They always giggled when they played together. **6.** Then he placed a shirt and some socks into it. **7.** Her pin was sparkling too. **8.** They stay at the cabin on weekends. **9.** She put the slices in the salad.

Page 28: 1. B, **2.** F, **3.** C, **4.** H, **5.** C, **6.** J, **7.** B, **8.** F

◆ Lesson 3 Recognizing Antonyms

Page 29: 1. late, **2.** finish, **3.** old, **4.** first, **5.** big, **6.** full, **7.** happy, **8.** soft, **9.** rainy, **10.** finish, **11.** last, **12.** empty, **13.** late, **14.** soft, **15.** sad

Page 30: 1. tiny, **2.** long, **3.** apart, **4.** leave, **5.** same, **6.** add, **7.** go, **8.** solution, **9.** none, **10.** thick

Page 31: Possible answers: **1.** That book is easy to read. **2.** A tiny hummingbird hovered near the feeder. **3.** I forgot to return my library book. **4.** The athlete was strong after weeks of training. **5.** She exits through the front door. **6.** The car broke down in the middle of nowhere. **7.** He put a thin coat of varnish on the table. **8.** I left the house without my raincoat. **9.** My old shoes are more comfortable than my new ones. **10.** We water our lawn on odd days of the week.

Page 32: 1. B, **2.** J, **3.** C, **4.** G, **5.** C, **6.** H, **7.** A, **8.** G

◆ Lesson 4 Using Antonyms

Page 33: 1. wake, **2.** excited, **3.** end, **4.** clean, **5.** many, **6.** smooth, **7.** close, **8.** under, **9.** expensive, **10.** outside

Page 34: 1. antonyms, 2. antonyms, 3. antonyms, 4. synonyms, 5. antonyms, 6. antonyms, 7. antonyms, 8. antonyms, 9. synonyms, 10. synonyms

Page 35: Possible answers: 1. wet, dry, 2. built, wrecked, 3. short, long, 4. gave, received, 5. warm, cool, 6. tall, short, 7. quiet, noisy, 8. stop, go, 9. quick, slow, 10. sweet, sour

Page 36: 1. C, 2. G, 3. A, 4. H, 5. B, 6. H, 7. D, 8. J, 9. B, 10. H

◆ Lesson 5 Using Context Clues

Page 37: 1. necessary, 2. sewing, 3. emergency, 4. planned

Page 38: 1. simple, fancy, 2. active, lazy, 3. proud, modest, 4. bright, dull, 5. clumsy, nimble

Page 39: 1. courageous, 2. sleepy, 3. annoyed, 4. build, 5. signed up for, 6. sea storm, 7. sad, 8. mistake, 9. sent to other countries, 10. warm

Page 40: 1. A, 2. H, 3. B, 4. J

◆ Lesson 6 Using Context Clues

Page 41: 1. common sense, 2. social groups, 3. plants in the bean family, 4. valuable flower from the rain forest, 5. body part that grinds up food, 6. swings of the club, 7. claws, 8. man-made

Page 42: 1. smaller boat, 2. hate, 3. comfort, 4. healthy, 5. kind of tree frog, 6. change, 7. rude, 8. tricks, 9. hide, 10. big snowstorm

Page 43: Possible answers: 1. weak, 2. not allow, 3. very clean, 4. large jungle cats, 5. fun, 6. got used to, 7. someone who never sees other people, 8. man-made lake, 9. crushed, 10. very hard experience

Page 44: 1. B, 2. G, 3. A, 4. F

◆ Lesson 7 Spelling Words

Page 46: 1. cried, 2. tasty, 3. married, 4. tiring, 5. hiding, 6. tried, 7. hurried, 8. driving, 9. cherries, 10. stating

Page 47: 1. sign, 2. wrong, 3. climb, 4. hour, 5. knee, 6. buy, 7. weak, 8. right, 9. rode, 10. through

Page 48: 1. Could, 2. living, 3. sea, 4. pale, 5. half, 6. its, 7. raking, 8. through
1. their, 2. leaving, 3. caring, 4. their, 5. loving, 6. taking, 7. babies, 8. families

◆ Lesson 8 Spelling Words

Page 49: 1. ie, 2. ei, 3. ie, 4. ei, 5. ie, 6. ei, 7. ie, 8. ie

Page 50: 1. planning, 2. ripped, 3. shopping, 4. funny, 5. slimmer, 6. grabbed, 7. digging, 8. tapping, 9. sunny, 10. canned

Page 51: Possible answers: 1. Wolves prey on rodents. 2. Our family eats three loaves of bread each week. 3. The elves helped the shoemaker make shoes. 4. The police caught the two thieves. 5. Can you put the tent up by yourselves? 6. Put the dishes on the shelves in the cupboard. 7. Some people believe that a cat has nine lives. 8. I raked leaves in the yard. 9. Sharp knives are safer to use than dull ones. 10. I have many different colored scarves.

Page 52: 1. great, 2. There, 3. Its, 4. should, 5. bare, 6. too, 7. skinny, 8. drippy, 9. signs, 10. whether
1. Right, 2. you're, 3. moving, 4. see, 5. made, 6. bigger, 7. They're, 8. believe, 9. great, 10. hotter

◆ Unit 1 Assessment

Page 54: 1. D, 2. G, 3. C, 4. J, 5. A, 6. J, 7. B, 8. H, 9. B, 10. J, 11. C, 12. G, 13. C, 14. F, 15. C, 16. G, 17. C, 18. J

◆ Unit 2 Recalling Information

Page 57: carnival
Directions will vary.

Page 58: 1. He brought the mail in from the mailbox. 2. He took off his coat and hung it up. 3. He checked the answering machine for new messages. 4. He read the paper.
1, 3, 4, 6, 5, 2
Answers will vary.

Answer Key *continued*

◆ Lesson 1 Recognizing Details

Page 59: 1. C, **2.** J, **3.** B, **4.** H

Page 60: 1. They sting to defend themselves. **2.** The bee dies a few hours later. **3.** Drones have no stingers. **4.** Men wear skirts sometimes in Scotland and Greece. **5.** They are called kilts. **6.** The guards outside of the Greek parliament building wear kilts.

Page 61: Possible answers: **1.** Ducks have short wings so they can dive underwater. **2.** They have long necks for catching food. **3.** Their webbed feet make good paddles for swimming. **4.** They have a gland under their tails that gives off waxy oil.

Possible answers: **5.** Older men sat on one side and young men on the other. **6.** Boys could not sit near girls. **7.** Most of the boys sat on the stairs. **8.** There was a special guard to make sure that children didn't talk.

Page 62: 1. C, **2.** J, **3.** C, **4.** G, **5.** C, **6.** F

◆ Lesson 2 Recalling Details

Page 63: 1. C, **2.** F, **3.** D

Page 64: Possible answers: **1.** The World's Fair was held in New York City. **2.** The World's Fair was held in 1964. **3.** It was a huge chunk of cheddar. **4.** The cheese weighed more than thirty-four thousand pounds. **5.** The human tongue can taste four flavors. **6.** Tongues have taste buds. **7.** Taste buds react to chemicals in food. **8.** They send signals to the brain.

Page 65: 1. Sloths live in rain forests in Brazil. **2.** They eat leaves, buds, and twigs. **3.** They use their long, curved claws. **4.** The Dutch call their wooden shoes *klompen.* **5.** Dutch people live in Holland. **6.** The land in Holland is below sea level. **7.** The Dutch people wore wooden shoes to keep their feet dry.

Page 66: 1. C, **2.** J, **3.** A, **4.** G, **5.** B, **6.** J

◆ Lesson 3 Identifying Sequence

Page 67: 1. C, **2.** H, **3.** B

Page 68: Possible answers: **2.** Place the sand and lime on the soil. **3.** Place a layer of stones held together with clay and cement. **4.** Place a layer of waterproofing. **5.** Place a layer made of lime, sand, earth, and brick.
2. In late spring cowhands corral the wild ponies. **3.** They send ponies to special trainers called bronco busters. **4.** Bronco busters put ponies through a training called "breaking" or "busting." **5.** Cowhands use ponies to round up cattle.

Page 69: 1. The sand gets very hot from the sun. **2.** The air near the ground rushes upward. **3.** The rush of air pulls more air behind it. **4.** Air currents wrap around the rising air and spin around it. **5.** It spins across the desert.

Page 70: 3, 1, 2, 4
3, 2, 4, 1

◆ Lesson 4 Recognizing Sequence

Page 71: 1. C, **2.** G, **3.** C, **4.** F

Page 72: 1. B, **2.** D, **3.** E, **4.** C, **5.** A
1. B, **2.** D, **3.** A, **4.** E, **5.** C

Page 73: 1. King Ethelred had to flee because London was attacked by Danes. **2.** Olaf brought ships to London to help the king. **3.** Olaf tied ropes to the stakes that held the bridge up. **4.** The men rowed as hard as they could. **5.** King Ethelred returned to the throne.

Page 74: 1. C, **2.** J, **3.** B, **4.** F, **5.** D

◆ Lesson 5 Stated Concepts

Page 75: 1. D, **2.** H, **3.** B, **4.** H

Page 76: 1. stated, **2.** stated, **3.** stated, **4.** not stated, **5.** stated, **6.** stated, **7.** stated, **8.** not stated, **9.** stated, **10.** not stated

Page 77: Possible answers: 1. The first movies did not have sound. They lasted only a few minutes. **2.** They might show people fighting. **3.** It was about the life of a fireman. **4.** A player threw the ball twenty-five feet. **5.** Knute Rockne was the first player famous for a passing game. **6.** The team's passing confused the other teams.

Page 78: 1. C, **2.** G, **3.** D, **4.** F, **5.** C

◆ Lesson 6 Recalling Stated Concepts

Page 79: 1. C, **2.** F, **3.** D, **4.** G, **5.** D

Page 80: 1. People use simple tools. **2.** People who lived in caves were the first people to make tools. **3.** They made tools out of stones. **4.** They had to live near animals. **5.** They could farm. **6.** It was called the Iron Age.

Page 81: 1. People used rubber to make balls. **2.** not stated, **3.** not stated, **4.** Tires are made from rubber. **5.** not stated

Page 82: 1. B, **2.** J, **3.** B, **4.** H, **5.** C

◆ Unit 2 Assessment

Page 84: 1. B, **2.** F, **3.** A, **4.** J, **5.** C, **6.** J, **7.** A, **8.** G, **9.** A, **10.** G, **11.** C, **12.** F

◆ Unit 3 Graphic Information

Page 87: 1–5 Answers will vary.

Time Lines: Answers will vary.

◆ Lesson 1 Identifying Signs

Page 89: 1. F, pedestrian crossing, **2.** J, railroad crossing, **3.** G, bus stop, **4.** B, telephone, **5.** A, camping, **6.** I, no U-turn, **7.** E, no left turn, **8.** C, do not enter, **9.** D, hospital, **10.** H, no trucks

Page 90: 1. merge, **2.** divided highway, **3.** signal ahead, **4.** hill, **5.** slippery when wet, **6.** bicycle route, **7.** pedestrian crossing, **8.** cattle crossing, **9.** deer crossing, **10.** farm machinery

Page 91: 1. G, **2.** B, **3.** C, **4.** A, **5.** H, **6.** D, **7.** E, **8.** I, **9.** J, **10.** F

Page 92: 1. C, **2.** C, **3.** B, **4.** B, **5.** A, **6.** B, **7.** B, **8.** A, **9.** B, **10.** B

◆ Lesson 2 Reading Maps

Page 93: 1. River Road, **2.** 8 miles, **3.** Park Avenue, **4.** 2 miles, **5.** Park Place, **6.** 8 miles, **7.** State Street, **8.** Park Avenue

Page 94: 1. information, **2.** Fish Food Shop, **3.** Dolphin Show, **4.** 200 yards, **5.** 300 yards, **6.** 200 yards, **7.** B3, **8.** A3, **9.** Shark Alley, **10.** Turtle Island

Page 95: 1. Helena, **2.** State Road, **3.** National Interstate Highway, **4.** 20 miles, **5.** 80 miles, **6.** 11, **7.** E4, **8.** State Road 200, National Interstate Highway 90, **9.** State Roads 83 and 200, National Interstate Highway 90, **10.** C1—Hamilton, B1—Missoula, C4—Helena, E4—Sheridan

Page 96: 1. D5, **2.** A1, **3.** C4, **4.** D4, **5.** D1, **6.** D3, **7.** A2, **8.** B2, **9.** D2, **10.** C1, **11.** B, **12.** C

◆ Lesson 3 Using Graphs

Page 97: 1. Finland, **2.** New Zealand, **3.** Finland, **4.** Sweden, **5.** Italy

Page 98: 1. 1950, **2.** 1960, 1970, **3.** 6,500,000, **4.** 4,750,000, **5.** 1980

Page 99: 1. 26 million; bar graph, **2.** 35%; circle graph, **3.** 23 million; bar graph, **4.** Licensing and Other Sources; bar or circle graph, **5.** Ticket Sales; bar or circle graph

Page 100: 1. A, **2.** H, **3.** A, **4.** G, **5.** D, **6.** H

◆ Lesson 4 Using Graphs

Page 101: 1. circle graph, **2.** line graph, **3.** bar graph, **4.** Graph B, **5.** Basketball, **6.** 6–8

Page 102: 1. Week 3, **2.** 10 hours, **3.** 25 hours, **4.** 25 hours, **5.** Weeks 1 and 4, **6.** Week 4

Page 103: 1. 45%, **2.** C, **3.** Graph B, **4.** B, **5.** line graph or bar graph

Page 104: 1. C, **2.** B, **3.** A, **4.** B, **5.** A, **6.** B

◆ Lesson 5 Consumer Materials

Page 105: 1. G, **2.** D, **3.** J, **4.** L, **5.** B, **6.** E, **7.** I, **8.** A, **9.** F, **10.** H, **11.** C, **12.** K

Page 106: Letters will vary.

Page 107: 1. Office Assistant, **2.** Campden Agency, **3.** Ms. Sorrell, **4.** type 60 words per minute, **5.** $8.50 per hour, **6.** Complete medical and dental plan, **7.** greet customers, answer phones, prepare estimates, **8.** 9 to 5, **9.** Monday through Friday, **10.** Letters will vary.

Page 108: 1. C, **2.** G, **3.** A, **4.** G, **5.** D, **6.** H, **7.** D, **8.** F, **9.** C, **10.** J

◆ Lesson 6 Consumer Materials

Page 109: 1. yes, **2.** no, **3.** yes, **4.** no, **5.** yes, **6.** no, **7.** yes, **8.** no, **9.** no, **10.** no, **11.** yes, **12.** yes, **13.** no, **14.** yes, **15.** no, **16.** no, **17.** yes, **18.** yes

Page 110: 1–5 Answers will vary.

Page 111: Applications will vary.

Page 112: 1. C, **2.** G, **3.** B, **4.** H, **5.** D

◆ Unit 3 Review

Page 113: Signs: Baggage claim area
Maps: 100 miles
Graphs: 15%
Consumer Materials: 10–2 Monday, Wednesday, Friday; medical benefits, paid vacation, pay increase after 90 days

◆ Unit 3 Assessment

Page 114: 1. B, **2.** J, **3.** A, **4.** H, **5.** C, **6.** J, **7.** C, **8.** F, **9.** D, **10.** H, **11.** D, **12.** G, **13.** A, **14.** H, **15.** C, **16.** G, **17.** A, **18.** H

◆ Unit 4 Constructing Meaning

Page 117: Possible answers: friend: fun, honest, agreeable, kind; employee: loyal, on time, organized, responsible; teacher: patient, calm, knowledgeable, fair
Sentences will vary.

Page 118: Answers will vary.

◆ Lesson 1 Recognizing Character Traits

Page 119: Possible answers: **1.** helpful, supportive, **2.** brave, peace-loving, **3.** artistic, creative, **4.** inventive, wise, intelligent, **5.** adventurous, bold

Page 120: 1. B, **2.** J, **3.** D, **4.** G

Page 121: Possible answers: **1.** clever, creative, **2.** independent, **3.** brave, **4.** resourceful, **5.** shy

Page 122: 1. B, **2.** F, **3.** B, **4.** G, **5.** C

◆ Lesson 2 Recognizing Character Traits

Page 123: Possible answers: **1.** loyal, **2.** peace-loving, **3.** compassionate

Page 124: 1. C, **2.** J, **3.** B, **4.** H, **5.** D

Page 125: Possible answers: **1.** brave, **2.** clever, **3.** charming, **4.** creative, **5.** talented

Page 126: 1. B, **2.** G, **3.** A, **4.** G, **5.** C

◆ Lesson 3 Identifying Main Idea

Page 127: C

Page 128: 1. main idea, **2.** detail, **3.** detail, **4.** main idea

Page 129: Possible answers: **1.** Different birds eat different kinds of foods. **2.** Allosaurus was a meat-eating dinosaur. **3.** Doughnuts didn't always have holes. **4.** Elevators are simple machines.

Page 130: 1. C, **2.** J, **3.** C, **4.** G

◆ Lesson 4 Finding the Main Idea

Page 131: 1. C, **2.** J

Page 132: 1. main idea, **2.** detail, **3.** detail, **4.** main idea, **5.** main idea

Page 133: Possible answers: **1.** People and animals can communicate without words. **2.** Animals use their tails in different ways. **3.** Wolves live in family groups. **4.** An orchestra is made up of four main types of instruments.

Page 134: 1. D, **2.** H, **3.** C

◆ Lesson 5 Comparing and Contrasting

Page 135: 1. C, **2.** C

Page 136: 1. a kangaroo rat and a rat kangaroo, **2.** Both are about a foot long, hop

Answer Key *continued*

on long back legs, have a head like a rat, and have a long tail. **3.** Both, **4.** But, **5.** The rat kangaroo has a pouch, the kangaroo rat does not.

Page 137: Likenesses: Both are alive, grow, and respond to light and water. Differences: Plants respond more slowly to the world around them. Animals are not rooted to one spot. Animals find food. Animals eat solid food. Plants make their own food.

Page 138: 1. C, **2.** G, **3.** A, **4.** F, **5.** D

◆ Lesson 6 Comparing and Contrasting

Page 139: 1. B, **2.** J, **3.** B

Page 140: 1. comets and meteors, **2.** Both are bright white. **3.** The white of a comet comes from reflected light. The light of a meteor comes from heat. **4.** Meteors fall to the earth, comets stay in space. **5.** On the other hand

Page 141: Marine Dolphins: mammal, home—oceans, snout—three inches long, size—thirty feet, food—fish and shellfish, sight—see well
River Dolphins: mammal, home—rivers, snout—one foot long, size—five to eight feet, food—fish and shellfish, sight—almost blind

Page 142: 1. D, **2.** F, **3.** B, **4.** H, **5.** D

◆ Lesson 7 Drawing Conclusions

Page 143: 1. B, **2.** F, **3.** D

Page 144: 1. Possible conclusion: Origami is popular everywhere. **2.** good conclusion, **3.** Possible conclusion: Sideburns were named after a Civil War General. **4.** good conclusion

Page 145: 1. Butterflies eat liquid food. **2.** Tom London is a talented actor. **3.** The trees produce more fruit of lesser quality. **4.** Plants need sunlight to grow.

Page 146: 1. C, **2.** F, **3.** B, **4.** J

◆ Lesson 8 Drawing Conclusions

Page 147: 1. A, **2.** G, **3.** D

Page 148: 1. valid, **2.** Several explorers have claimed to be the first to reach the North Pole. **3.** Spiders control the insect population. **4.** Grasses are an important part of the human diet.

Page 149: 1. Hot air rises. **2.** All deserts are dry. **3.** Royal children are taught more than academic subjects.

Page 150: 1. C, **2.** G, **3.** D, **4.** H

◆ Lesson 9 Drawing Conclusions

Page 151: 1. B, **2.** H, **3.** B

Page 152: 1. invalid, **2.** valid, **3.** invalid, **4.** invalid

Page 153: Possible answers: **1.** Many members of the elephant family care for the young. **2.** Annie Peck was brave and determined. **3.** Some words do not reflect their original meaning.

Page 154: 1. C, **2.** F, **3.** A, **4.** H

◆ Lesson 10 Recognizing Cause and Effect

Page 155: 1. C, **2.** G, **3.** A

Page 156: 1. He liked to dress in fancy clothes. **2.** They grow well on the forest floor. **3.** Your eyes have tears at all times. **4.** Hair gives people and animals warmth and protection.

Page 157: 1. They eat a good diet, get a lot of fresh air and exercise, and live in a hot climate. **2.** These foods are easily found in their environment. **3.** The constant motion of the ocean waves makes sand. **4.** Beaches would be covered with sharp rocks, pebbles, and shells instead of sand.

Page 158: 1. C, **2.** J, **3.** D, **4.** G

◆ Lesson 11 Understanding Cause and Effect

Page 159: 1. D, **2.** G, **3.** C

Page 160: 1. In the 1500s, tulips were rare. **2.** Fish swim in large groups. **3.** People took few baths. **4.** Owls see well in the dark. **5.** Game birds can't see them.

Page 161: 1. The center of the tree must be rotten. **2.** People cut down older pine forests. **3.** They cut them down for wood. **4.** They used sharp sticks to hunt and dig. **5.** They could sharpen their sticks with knives.

Page 162: 1. C, **2.** G, **3.** B, **4.** F

◆ Lesson 12 Recognizing Cause and Effect

Page 163: 1. effect, **2.** cause, **3.** cause, **4.** effect, **5.** cause

Page 164: 1. They thought any odd sounds made at night were made by Pan. **2.** The back of a cat's eye eyes reflects light. **3.** You can tell direction by the growth on a tree.

Page 165: 1. The heat from the soup flows into the spoon. **2.** Metal gets hot very quickly. **3.** Plastic does not conduct heat well. **4.** The heat from a stove would heat a metal handle. **5.** Wood doesn't conduct heat well.

Page 166: 1. C, **2.** F, **3.** D, **4.** J

◆ Lesson 13 Summarizing and Paraphrasing

Page 167: 1. C, **2.** Answers will vary.

Page 168: Possible answers: **1.** Some wild animals are small and weak. However, they aren't helpless because they develop other life skills. **2.** Bald eagles really aren't bald. The white feathers on their head make them look bald from a distance. **3.** Moonbows appear after a night rain. The light from a bright moon makes them show up. **4.** Hundreds of years ago jesters entertained kings. **5.** Stars are made of glowing gases. Planets are solid bodies smaller than stars.

Page 169: Possible answers: **1.** Our supply of natural fuels is limited. Scientists are trying to find new fuels. **2.** Earth's ice ages were a result of reduced heat and light from the sun. **3.** In ancient times, people used nonstandard units to measure things. **4.** The Puritans who settled in New England in the 1600s had strict laws about what people could not do on Sundays. These laws were called Blue Laws.

Page 170: 1. B, **2.** J, **3.** A

◆ Lesson 14 Summarizing and Paraphrasing

Page 171: C

Page 172: Possible answers: **1.** Your shoe size is based on a measurement devised by an English king. **2.** Because of the rough seas around it, explorers called the tip of Africa the Cape of Storms. The king of Portugal changed the name to the Cape of Good Hope. **3.** Two hundred million-year-old dinosaur prints can be found in the rocks of the Connecticut River Valley.

Page 173: Possible answers: **1.** Weeds are not good for garden plants. They take water and sunlight from other plants. They can also choke the life out of plants. **2.** The oldest diamond in the world is in the crown of the queen of England. It is called Kohinoor, "mountain of light." **3.** In 1555, a servant, Nizam, saved his king's life. As a reward, the king said Nizam could be king for six hours. During his short reign, Nizam gave money to the poor and had a special coin made.

Page 174: 1. D, **2.** G, **3.** C

◆ Unit 4 Assessment

Page 176: 1. A, **2.** J, **3.** C, **4.** G, **5.** B, **6.** F, **7.** B, **8.** J, **9.** D, **10.** H

◆ Unit 5 Extending Meaning

Page 179: Answers will vary.

Page 180: Answers and sentences will vary.

◆ Lesson 1 Predicting Outcomes

Page 181: 1. A, **2.** B, **3.** C

Page 182: 1. C, **2.** C, **3.** C, **4.** B

Page 183: 1. Max filled the glass with water. **2.** Jana called Sue. **3.** Bill checked the bulletin board. **4.** Keith turned on the television. **5.** Carmen took pictures of her new friends.

Page 184: 1. B, **2.** F, **3.** A, **4.** J

Answer Key *continued*

◆ Lesson 2 Predicting Outcomes

Page 185: Prediction: Dolores won the election.
Story Clues: Barb backed her car but didn't hear the sound of glass crunching under the tires.
Experience Clues: Glass punctures tires.
Prediction: Barb has a flat tire.

Page 186: 1. Paulo got an A in math. **2.** Jack and Jesse started riding their bikes. **3.** Tina went for a walk along the busy streets of New York. **4.** Bob realized that the car will probably break down in a short while.

Page 187: 1. Hannah gets the job. **2.** Dave burns the bread. **3.** Mr. Lee gets lost. **4.** Jane's pictures don't turn out.

Page 188: 1. C, **2.** G, **3.** C

◆ Lesson 3 Identifying Fact and Opinion

Page 189: 1. Red and yellow are colors. **2.** Dog and cats are mammals. **3.** Fossils can be found on Earth. **4.** Vincent van Gogh painted the still-life "Sunflowers." **5.** Tivoli Gardens is one of the world's oldest amusement parks. **6.** Sewage and chemicals from factories cause water pollution. **7.** Maps show distance and direction. **8.** All citizens of the United States have rights.

Page 190: 1. fact, **2.** fact, **3.** fact, **4.** opinion, **5.** opinion, **6.** fact, **7.** opinion, **8.** fact, **9.** fact, **10.** opinion, **11.** fact

Page 191: 1. F, **2.** F, **3.** F, **4.** O, **5.** F, **6.** O, **7.** F, **8.** O, **9.** F, **10.** O

Page 192: 1. B, **2.** H, **3.** A, **4.** G, **5.** B, **6.** H

◆ Lesson 4 Identifying Fact and Opinion

Page 193: 1. F, O, **2.** F, O, **3.** O, F, **4.** O, F, **5.** F, O

Page 194: 1. Fact, **2.** Opinion, think, **3.** Fact, **4.** Fact, **5.** Fact, **6.** Opinion, feel, **7.** Fact, **8.** Opinion, easy, **9.** Fact, **10.** Opinion, to me, **11.** Fact, **12.** Fact, **13.** Opinion, most awkward, **14.** Fact, **15.** Fact

Page 195: 1. F, **2.** F, **3.** O, **4.** F, **5.** O, **6.** F, **7.** O, **8.** F, **9.** O, **10.** F, **11.** O, **12.** F, **13.** F, **14.** O, **15.** F

Page 196: 1. C, **2.** G, **3.** A, **4.** G, **5.** D, **6.** G

◆ Lesson 5 Applying Passage Elements

Page 197: 1. B, **2.** A

Page 198: 1. A, **2.** C, **3.** C, **4.** B

Page 199: 1. Basketball has changed over the years. **2.** People who are born in the morning tend to be early birds. **3.** Dolphins come to the surface to breathe.

Page 200: 1. C, **2.** G, **3.** B, **4.** F

◆ Lesson 6 Applying Passage Elements

Page 201: 1. C, **2.** B, **3.** C, **4.** A

Page 202: 1. C, **2.** B, **3.** C

Page 203: 1. Citrus fruits are a good source of Vitamin C. **2.** Horses were not found in North America before the 1500s. **3.** Cashmere is costly because it is rare and hard to obtain.

Page 204: 1. C, **2.** G, **3.** C, **4.** H

◆ Unit 5 Assessment

Page 206: 1. A, **2.** H, **3.** D, **4.** G, **5.** D, **6.** F, **7.** B, **8.** F, **9.** B, **10.** G